BASICS
FASHION DESIGN

Research and Design for Fashion

Third edition

Fairchild Books
An imprint of Bloomsbury Publishing Plc

BLOOMSBURY
LONDON · OXFORD · NEW YORK · NEW DELHI · SYDNEY

Fairchild Books
An imprint of Bloomsbury Publishing Plc

Imprint previously known as AVA

50 Bedford Square   1385 Broadway
London   New York
WC1B 3DP   NY 10018
UK   USA

www.bloomsbury.com

**FAIRCHILD BOOKS, BLOOMSBURY and the Diana logo
are trademarks of Bloomsbury Publishing Plc**

First edition published by AVA Publishing SA, 2007
Second edition published by AVA Publishing SA, 2012
This 3rd edition is published by Fairchild Books, an imprint of Bloomsbury Publishing Plc
Copyright © Bloomsbury Publishing Plc, 2017

Simon Seivewright and Richard Sorger have asserted their right under the Copyright,
Designs and Patents Act, 1988, to be identified as Authors of this work.

British Library Cataloguing-in-Publication Data
A catalogue record for this book is available from the British Library.

ISBN: PB: 978-1-4742-4636-1
          ePDF: 978-1-4742-4637-8

Library of Congress Cataloging-in-Publication Data
Names: Seivewright, Simon, author. | Sorger, Richard.
Title: Research and Design for Fashion / Simon Seivewright and Richard Sorger.
Description: Third edition. | New York : Fairchild Books, 2017. | Series:
Basics fashion design | Includes bibliographical references and index.
Identifiers: LCCN 2016001549| ISBN 9781474246361 (paperback) | ISBN
9781474246378 (epdf)
Subjects: LCSH: Fashion design. | Fashion design—Study and teaching. |
BISAC: DESIGN / Fashion.
Classification: LCC TT507 .S425 2016 | DDC 746.9/2076—dc23 LC record available
at http://lccn.loc.gov/2016001549

Cover image by Olivia Overton
Cover design by Louise Dugdale
Typeset by Lachina
Printed and bound in China

**An Alexander McQueen
dress for the Spring/
Summer 2015
collection.**

Contents

4

Designing from your research 101

5

Communicating your ideas 147

Maison Martin Margiela
haute couture
Spring/Summer 2015

Research is vital to any design process, as it will provide you with the foundations with which to build and develop your desired creative outcomes. Research involves the initial hunt and collection of ideas prior to design. It should be an experimental process; an investigation to find out or support your knowledge of a particular subject, market, consumer, innovation, or technology.

Research is an essential tool in the creative process and is one that will provide you with information and creative direction, as well as a narrative to a collection. Research is about a journey of discovery that can often take weeks or even months to collate and process. It is also a very personal activity, which provides the viewer with an insight into the thinking, aspirations, interests, and creative vision of the designer.

By conducting in-depth and broad-ranging research, a designer can begin to interpret a series of garments or to evolve a collection. Silhouettes, textures and fabrics, colors, details, prints and embellishments, and market and consumer all have their place in the process of design and are found or directed by the research gathered.

This new edition of *Research and Design for Fashion* leads you through the essential stages of research and the translation of these stages into fashion design ideas. It discusses crucial elements in the research and design process, such as the brief and the constraints that it can sometimes impose. It explains the importance of identifying both your target market and customer, and of understanding the different levels and genres of fashion before setting out on the creative research itself. It then discusses the many possible avenues for research and the need to set a theme, concept, or narrative to your collection.

You then explore how to translate your research into early design ideas, looking at both 2D and 3D approaches. The book provides useful exercises for you to do that explain how to bridge the gap between the research and design outcomes. Design and collection development is broken down into a series of elements that then provide a foundation for expanding your ideas into a well-considered, cohesive, and balanced collection. Finally, the book shows and explores a variety of approaches to communicating and rendering your design work.

Interviews at the end of each chapter, featuring established international fashion designers, a trend forecasting agency, and fashion educators will inspire you on your creative journey throughout the book, and provide you with valuable insights into what it means to get into, work in, and succeed in the fashion industry.

Research and Design for Fashion will provide you with the basic fundamental skills and knowledge that you need to start you on your journey of designing an in-depth, innovative, and creative collection all of your own. Good luck— and above all, enjoy the discovery of the creative design process!

Sadly, the original author of this book, Simon Seivewright, died in 2013.

> **"I get my ideas out of my dreams . . . if you're lucky enough to use something you see in a dream, it is purely original. It's not in the world—it's in your head. I think that is amazing."**
> Alexander McQueen, British fashion designer, 1969–2010

Research—what and why?

1

Research is about creative investigation, and it is about recording information for use now or in the future. But what exactly is research? Designers are constantly looking for new ideas, as fashion by its very nature is always changing and reinventing itself. But where does it all start?

In this first chapter, we aim to demystify what research is, as well as to explore the process of creative investigation a little further. We will also look at why you should research in the first place. The chapter discusses what a brief is, the different types of briefs that exist, and what it is that the designer is being asked to do.

What do you need to consider as a designer before you begin work on any project or collection? This is a question that every designer should ask herself or himself. Later in the chapter, we will explore what the purpose of research is and what precisely it should contain in terms of information.

> "Research is what I'm doing when I don't know what I'm doing."
> Wernher von Braun

Above all, the process of research should be fun, exciting, informative, and (most importantly) useful. This chapter will help you discover how you can make it all of these things!

Japanese scene created by the master Kunisada, circa 1853.

What is a brief?

The brief is usually the start to any creative project, and the project is a sustained body of work that is normally time-bound. The purpose of a brief is essentially to inspire you and to outline the aims and objectives that are required. It will identify any constraints, conditions, or problems that need to be solved. In addition, it will provide you with information on what final outcomes or tasks are to be achieved. The brief is there to help you and more importantly to guide the whole research and design process.

Types of briefs

There are several types of briefs. The most common one is found within the academic forum where it is usually set by the tutor and asks you as an individual to respond to it. The aims are what you are expected to learn, and the objectives will be the work demonstrated. As the student, you will be expected to answer not only the brief's creative requirements, but also the assessment criteria that will be clearly identified. The tutor uses the brief as an important tool to help teach specific skills and develop and improve your knowledge and understanding. It also sets creative boundaries.

A further type of brief also found within the academic forum is one for a competition. It often is set by a company or external organization as a way of promoting products or a brand and in turn encouraging new talent within the industry. This association with industry will often provide sponsorship, placement awards, and travel awards for the students taking part.

Commercial briefs and client-based briefs are the other types you will come across as a designer. They will have very specific aims and objectives that will consider some or all of the following: market, season, genres, cost, and occasion. The true measure of your creativity as a designer will be to achieve something exciting and innovative while considering very closely what it is that you are being asked to produce and adhering to the constraints of the brief in order to achieve the client's approval.

Another common type of brief is one that asks you to work within a team—for example, a large high-street brand. Here you will be expected to work with others on a project, and you will have specific tasks assigned to you that will ultimately work toward presenting a coherent and cohesive collection.

Working to a commercial brief

A good example of a designer working to a commercial brief is supplied by British designer Julien Macdonald, who redesigned the British Airways uniform. In this case the brief would have had very specific criteria and restrictions on design, use of fabric, cost, function, and performance.

What was the brief British Airways set for you?
I was asked along with many other designers to come up with a set of sketches for uniforms that could be worn by all the different British Airways staff from all over the world. The uniforms had to be functional pieces that could be worn by the cabin crew to the ground staff to the baggage handlers, over 80,000 employees worldwide.

The designs were submitted anonymously to the British Airways board of directors and design team so that the ideas would not be judged on the name of the designer. They were really surprised when they found out that the clean, simple, stylish ideas were mine, as they associated my name with glitz and glamour!

What constraints did you face?
There were many complex constraints, as the investment by the company was worth millions of pounds and the last time it was changed was over ten years ago, when Paul Costelloe did the designs. The clothes had to fit from a size 6 to 22, be for both men and women, and there was to be no discrimination between race, color, or creed. The garments had to be in the same fabric, whether you were working in a Russian winter or the summer in the Seychelles.

I spent time working alongside the staff to find out about their working lives—from leaving their homes to going to work to then arriving in a hotel after a ten-hour flight and having to wash the blouse in the sink to have it fresh for the return flight the next morning! The garments were given a pilot period where we looked at how they performed under normal working conditions. For example, did the fabric wear well? Did the buttons fall off? The final garments were then success-fully put into production and can be seen on any current flight with British Airways.

What's in a brief?

Occasion and season
As a designer, I believe it is important to be aware of whether you are designing for a specific occasion or season, which will have an impact on many of the design factors, such as fabric and color.

Muse or customer
A brief will sometimes ask you to design for a very specific consumer of a certain age, size, and gender. It may also ask you to build a customer profile and to consider elements such as background, work, lifestyle, and income.

Target market
A brief will often ask you to focus on a specific market sector in the industry, such as high street or middle-market price points. This again requires you to consider market analysis and customer profiling.

Material and fabric
Sometimes in the academic field, you will be asked to problem solve a brief that focuses your creativity on the use of a particular type or quality of fabric, for example, jersey.

Costing
Most project briefs, whether they are academic or industry set, will require you to consider the price that something will cost to produce.

Practical outcomes
These are simply what you are expected to produce. The brief may have a specific garment type as its final outcome—a dress, a jacket, or a piece of knitwear, for example.

What is research?

Fashion by its very definition is about current popular custom or style; fashion designers express the zeitgeist, or spirit of the times, in their work. Fashion is constantly changing and designers are expected to reinvent the wheel every season. Because of this constant pressure for the new, designers have to dig ever deeper and search ever further for new inspiration and ways of interpreting this into their collections. Fashion designers are obsessive collectors always on the hunt for new and exciting things to inspire them. So the need to gather and source material for use in the creative process is essential for feeding the imagination.

Three types of research

Research is about investigation—learning about something new or learning about something from the past. It can often be likened to the beginning of a journey of exploration. It is about reading, visiting, or perhaps viewing, but above all, it is about recording information.

There are three types of research. The first type is the visual inspiration for the collection, and this will often help to set the theme, mood, or concept that is essential in developing an identity for your creative work. The second is gathering and sourcing the tangible and practical materials for your collection—for example, fabric, trims, and buttons. The third is perhaps the most important aspect, as it relates to the consumer and market that you are creating the design work for. The brief may already state the market, but it is essential that you, as a designer, explore and identify who you are designing for and understand their lifestyle and interests. You also need to research the broader market and competitors within it.

Undertaking all three aspects of research will give you a much more solid foundation upon which to build your design ideas. Your research should always be broad ranging and in depth, enabling you to innovate, rather than to simply imitate in the collection that you create from it.

Research could be likened to a diary or journal, a snapshot of who you are, what you are interested in, and what is happening in the world at a specific time. Trends, along with social and political issues, could be documented as part of your research—as all these things have an impact on the research and creative design process. The information you compile in your research diary is likely to be useful both now and in the future.

What is the purpose of research?

You know what research is, but why do you need it? How does it help you as a designer?

Research is there, above all, to inspire you as a creative individual. It is a way of stimulating the mind and opening up new directions in design. By gathering different references and exploring many avenues of interest, you can begin to explore a variety of creative possibilities before you channel and focus your imagination toward a concept, theme, or direction for a collection.

Research will help you learn about a subject. You might discover information previously unknown to you, or perhaps you could explore new skills or technologies.

Research is an opportunity to inquire into your own interests and expand your awareness and knowledge of the world around you. As a result, research is very much a personal and individual task, and although a team of people can gather it, one person generally has the creative vision and takes the lead.

Research is a way of showing the world how you see it and how you think. And this is extremely important in differentiating you from everyone else in the industry. Think of it as a personal diary of a moment in your creative lifetime and a document to show whoever is interested what has inspired you and had an effect on your life.

The final point to remember is that research must above all else be inspiring and useful.

Example of research and early stage design ideas.

> **"Research is formalized curiosity. It is poking and prying with a purpose."**
> Zora Neale Hurston,
> American folklorist and writer,
> 1891–1960

What should research contain?

As you have already discovered, research is about the investigation and recording of information. You can break down this information usefully into a series of categories that will help inspire you and provide the different components of a collection's direction.

Shapes and structures

By its very definition, "shape" is an area or form with a definite outline and a visible appearance and structure. It is also the way in which something is constructed or supported in a framework. Shapes are a vital element of research and ultimately of design too, as they provide you with potential ideas to translate onto the body and into garments. Without shape, there would be no silhouettes in fashion design (see pages 108–110). To support shape, you also need to consider structure and how something is constructed or created. The potential to understand how a framework or parts can support shape is vital, and again this knowledge can be translated into fashion design. Consider the role of a domed roof of a cathedral, contemporary glasshouse, or the crinoline frame of a nineteenth-century dress, for example.

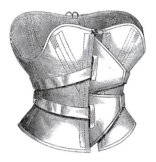

Crinoline

Crinoline is a lightweight frame constructed by connecting together horizontal hoops of wire or boning and cotton tape (boning is a flexible material originally made from whalebone, but now made from metal or plastic). Crinolines were worn under skirts to allow the silhouette of the body to be exaggerated. Their use was at its most popular and extreme in shape during the mid-to-late 1800s.

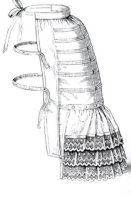

Historical examples of nineteenth-century crinolines and corsets used to exaggerate the human silhouette.

Reichstag Building, Germany. The internal structure shown in this image links closely with that of a nineteenth-century crinoline.

Reichstag Building, Germany.

Details

As a designer, you must consider inspiration not only for shape in your research, but also for the more practical elements like the details. The details of a garment can be anything from where the topstitching is placed to pocket types, fastenings, and shapes of cuffs and collars. The details of a garment are equally important to design, as is the silhouette, and these will often be the main selling feature once buyers give it closer examination. It is therefore essential that you incorporate detailing in order to create a successful and more evolved garment.

The research gathered for this element of the design process can come from many different sources. It may be that you explore the pockets and cuffs of a military jacket or take elements from a historical garment. It may be that the details come from a more abstract source; for example, a pocket shape may be inspired by something more organic. The inspiration for the detailing on a garment, or a whole collection, should filter through from all the different sources that you have researched. The detailing may not be immediately obvious, but as you will learn, it is an important part of the design process and must ultimately be considered.

Topstitching

Topstitching is any stitching visible on the right side of a garment. It can be decorative, but its main function is to reinforce a seam. It can commonly be seen in workwear or denim garments such as jeans.

Proenza Schouler Spring/Summer 2016.

Alexander McQueen Spring/Summer 2016.

Color

Color is a fundamental consideration in the research and design process. It is often the first element that is noticed about a design and influences how that garment or collection is perceived. Color has always fascinated humankind, and the use of color in our clothing reflects our personalities, characters, and taste. It can also convey significant messages reflecting different cultures and social status. In your designs, color is often the starting point of a collection and can dictate the mood and season that you are designing for. The research you gather for color should be both primary and secondary (see chapter 2) and should allow you to mix and play with a variety of combinations.

Where your inspiration comes from is limitless, as you are surrounded by color. Nature, for instance, provides an unlimited array of colors, tints, shades, and tones that you can translate into a palette for the design process. Equally, your inspiration could come from an artist, a specific painting, or a photograph.

Palette

A palette is a piece of board that an artist uses to mix paint before painting, but for a designer, it means a group of colors that are put together. They can coordinate, have similar hues and tones, or can be juxtaposed and clash. In chapter four, we will discuss color theory and the use of color palettes in the design of a collection.

Textures

Texture refers to the surface quality of objects and appeals to our sense of touch. Light and dark patterns of different textures can provide visual stimulation for viewers without their actually having to touch an object; these patterns also can describe the surface that is presented.

In fashion design, research into texture will ultimately lead to fabric and the many different qualities and finishes available to you (see chapter 4). The way that something looks and feels on the body is a crucial part of the design process, and inspiration for this can come from many different sources.

The textures you research can often inspire new ideas for surface manipulation, and the way that a fabric handles will help define and possibly shape a garment. Images of building materials, landscapes, and organic forms may help inspire knitwear and fabric manipulation techniques, such as pleating.

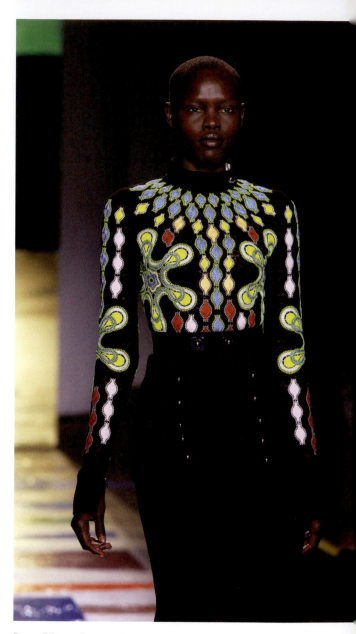

Peter Pilotto Autumn/Winter 2015.

An illustration by Ernst Haeckel from his book *Kunstformen der Natur* (*Artforms of Nature*) 1904.

OMO VALLEY ETHIOPIA

At the age of fifteen to sixteen a Mursi girl will have her lip
cut where a small clay plate is inserted causing the lip to stretch.
As she gets older she scarring can be used to accentuate her
female body. Symmetrical patterns around the hips, stomach and
breasts highlight the areas associated with fertility.

Research boards inspired by African tribal culture.

LOOK FIVE

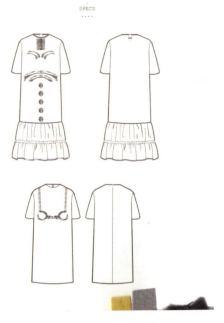

L O O K S I X

Print and surface decoration

Through the process of research, you may start to gather information and references that have natural patterns or decorations on them and that lend themselves to be interpreted into print and textile development. Images or objects may be decorative, jeweled, repeated, or mirrored; or they may provide an opportunity for a motif within a design concept.

Surface qualities may also suggest translation into textile techniques, such as embroidery, smocking, appliqué, and beading (see page 125). Surface finishes can be applied to a fabric or garment to alter the look or feel and perhaps reflect the mood of the source of inspiration. For example, distressing, ageing, and fading fabrics might be translated from scorched arid land in Africa; or jeweled and decorative qualities could be translated from insects, reptiles, or fish.

Designs inspired by African tribal culture.

Cultural influences

Cultural influences can be everything from the appreciation of literature, arts, and music from your own country to the appreciation of the customs and civilization of another. Looking at another country for ideas can provide you with a wealth of inspiration that may translate into color, fabric, print, and garment shapes. Designers such as Alexander McQueen, Jean Paul Gaultier, and John Galliano are well known for the way they look to different cultures as a springboard for their collections.

As a designer, you may be inspired by literature and employ this to provide a narrative to your collection; current exhibitions in museums and galleries may also have an influence on the research that you gather and what you design.

Detail of the oil "Las dos Fridas" ("The Two Fridas") by Mexican artist Frida Kahlo, 1939.

Jean Paul Gaultier Autumn/Winter 2005, Frida Kahlo–inspired and Mexican-inspired collections.

Japanese scene created by the master
Kunisada, circa 1853 (top). Christian Dior
haute couture Spring/Summer 2007. Designed
by John Galliano and inspired by Japanese
costume (bottom).

"It was interesting to explore historical clothes and to think about those textures, those embroideries, those materials and then to interpret them for a woman today, not as costume, but as wardrobe."
Nicolas Ghesquière

Historical influences

As with working in any creative field, it is essential to have an understanding of what has taken place in the past in order to move ideas and technologies forward. Historical influences may be found in any design discipline from any culture. They could be as diverse as looking at ancient tiles from an Islamic mosque to Japanese samurai armor.

A key element of historical research must be that of dress history or costume. Learning about dress history is an extremely important part of being a fashion designer, and for many, it has provided a treasure trove and wealth of information on everything from shape and tailoring to fabric and embellishment.

Vivienne Westwood describes the process of looking at historical dress for inspiration as "synthesizing the old into the new." She is well known for exploring many different periods of costume history to invigorate her collections. Fashion by its definition is about current popular trends, and so looking at costume provides you with an insight into trends of the past.

Portrait of Marie Antoinette by Elisabeth Louise Vigée Le Brun (1755–1842) showing the elaborate draping and detailing of the eighteenth century.

Christian Dior haute couture Autumn/Winter 2000. Designed by John Galliano and inspired by Marie Antoinette.

Contemporary trends

Having an awareness of events and cultural trends is something that you must develop as a designer. Observing global changes, social trends, and political climates is essential in creating clothes for a specific target market. Tracking trends is not necessarily a fully conscious activity, but merely an ability to tune in to the spirit of the times or zeitgeist. It also requires an awareness of subtle changes in taste and interests that often start out on the "street."

The "bubble-up effect" describes how activities, special interests, and subcultural groups have an influence on mainstream culture—often through music, exposure online, and on television—and are seen as a new direction for fashion and media.

Fashion forecasting agencies (see pages 138–139) and trend magazines (page 38) are just some of the ways in which you can easily gain access to this sort of information.

Tangible and material research

In addition to considering potential sources of visual inspiration, you will also find it essential to gather ideas for the more tangible and material components of a collection.

As a fashion designer, you are considering how the body is to be covered, wrapped, protected, decorated, and transformed. Therefore, working with and understanding materials is an essential part of that process. Tangible research at this early stage can simply be about discovering objects and items such as new and old fabrics, or antique buttons and trims, such as lace. A vintage garment could inspire a fabric manipulation, quality, or surface decoration. Objects you collect on a cultural visit might later provide you with ideas for shape, texture, and color, but might also inspire the concept, theme, or narrative of your research.

These more tangible objects can help you visualize their use and function in the design of a garment, and inspire you to develop ideas from them during the design process.

Flea markets are an excellent source of objects that might prove inspiring. These objects could be used to inspire shape, texture, and color, but might also inspire the concept, theme, or narrative of your research.

Who are you designing for?

It is important to consider your market (the third aspect of research) as early as possible, as it will often dictate and define where you should begin. As already discussed in "Types of briefs" (see page 2), it may well be that an externally set brief, provided by a client, company, or your tutor, outlines any constraints or market levels that you should be considering in the research and design process. Having a solid understanding of the customer and the competitors you are facing at the start of the project means that you will have a more focused and well-targeted collection in the end.

Identifying your market

Early market research could simply involve looking at examples of the advertising and brand identity, online presence, store layouts, and merchandise for a particular design, brand, or company that you feel falls in line with the customer you would like to design for. Brands will often have a clear muse or model type that defines their ideal customer or will perhaps create one that consumers will aspire to, promoted with the message, "if you dress in our garments, you too could look like this."

This early market research could take the form of collected promotional material, such as look books, online images, magazine advertisements, catwalk images, store photographs, window displays, packaging and logos, sketches of key garments, written information, company mission, and target customer statements.

This type of material can be collected across a range of brands within a certain market level to enable you to understand how competitors differentiate between one another and create a signature identity to their brand and designs. This type of research activity can often be described as shop/brand reporting.

Identifying a muse

You may wish to identify a muse of your own at this early stage of the process, as doing this can often help with the focus of who is going to wear your clothes. Having a muse or specific customer in mind allows you to refer to this person when designing the collection. Would that person wear this garment? How and when would the person wear it? Does it connect to and enhance that person and her or his own style or identity?

Designers will often have a particular model, actress, or singer that they feel epitomizes their brand—or at least they do for that season! Hubert de Givenchy famously worked with the actress Audrey Hepburn for many years, helping to create her iconic style. Another example is provided by Madonna, who over the years has been connected to designer brands such as Jean Paul Gaultier, Dolce and Gabbana, Versace, Louis Vuitton, and more recently Versace again for their Spring/Summer 2015 advertising campaign. Her strong personal identity and celebrity thereby become linked to that specific designer and the aspirations of the customer to purchase from that brand.

Hubert de Givenchy with Audrey Hepburn
in Paris, France, 1982.

Later on, we will look more closely at the
different market levels and genres within
fashion so that you better understand the
breadth of the industry and the market
that is potentially available to you as a
designer (pages 128–131).

"She gave the most to
fashion because of her
beauty and personality
. . . that marvelous face
and those strong little
shoulders."
Hubert de Givenchy
on Audrey Hepburn

Exercise 1

Brainstorming

In this chapter, you have learned about the importance of research and some of the key categories that it can fall into.

This exercise is designed to get you thinking laterally and broadly within the main research categories to develop possible avenues for visual, tangible, and market research.

Use dictionaries, a thesaurus, and the Internet to assist in this activity. Pictures can also be assigned to the words written down and therefore provide you with potential starting points for your collection and also possible ideas for a theme or concept.

Be open-minded and allow your imagination to wander into many different related and unrelated areas; the juxtaposition of words and themes can often present new concepts and marriages for the design.

Start by selecting one of the following visual research categories:

- shapes and structures
- details
- color
- textures
- print and embellishment
- historical influences
- cultural influences
- contemporary trends

Then think of something that might be connected or relate to that category— for example, red for the color category, or China for the cultural category, or geometric for shapes and structures, or the 1920s for the history category.

Using this first subject or topic, begin to branch out as many ideas, words, meanings, descriptions, places, and objects as you can. Make sure that you also start to add in references for the other research categories that may or may not relate to the first topic that you wrote down.

Remember: you can use a dictionary and thesaurus to help with words and meanings to branch away from the first word listed.

As you begin to develop a series of words and directions, add in ideas for possible tangible elements, such as objects, trims, or fabric types that could relate to and be sourced at the next stage. You could also start to think of people that could be associated with some of the ideas generated; these could be models, celebrities, actors, musicians, or even figures from history or literature.

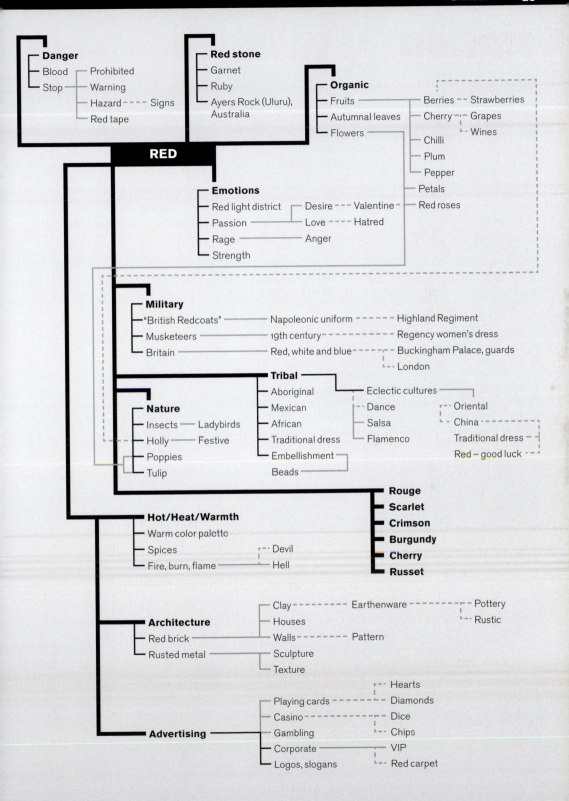

Danger
- Blood
- Stop
  - Prohibited
  - Warning
  - Hazard - - - Signs
  - Red tape

Red stone
- Garnet
- Ruby
- Ayers Rock (Uluru), Australia

Organic
- Fruits
  - Berries - - Strawberries
  - Cherry - - Grapes
    - Wines
- Autumnal leaves
- Flowers
  - Chilli
  - Plum
  - Pepper
  - Petals
  - Red roses

RED

Emotions
- Red light district
  - Desire - - - Valentine
- Passion
  - Love - - - Hatred
- Rage
  - Anger
- Strength

Military
- "British Redcoats" —— Napoleonic uniform - - - Highland Regiment
- Musketeers —— 19th century - - - Regency women's dress
- Britain —— Red, white and blue - - - Buckingham Palace, guards
  - London

Tribal
- Aboriginal
- Mexican
- African
- Traditional dress
- Embellishment
- Beads

- Eclectic cultures
- Dance
- Salsa
- Flamenco
  - Oriental
  - China
  - Traditional dress
  - Red – good luck

Nature
- Insects —— Ladybirds
- Holly —— Festive
- Poppies
- Tulip

Hot/Heat/Warmth
- Warm color palette
- Spices —— Devil
- Fire, burn, flame —— Hell

Rouge
Scarlet
Crimson
Burgundy
Cherry
Russet

Architecture
- Red brick
- Rusted metal
  - Clay - - - Earthenware - - - Pottery
    - Rustic
  - Houses
  - Walls - - - Pattern
  - Sculpture
  - Texture

Advertising
- Playing cards - - - Hearts
  - Diamonds
- Casino - - - Dice
- Gambling - - - Chips
- Corporate —— VIP
- Logos, slogans - - - Red carpet

Interview
Malene Oddershede Bach

Danish-born London-based designer Malene Oddershede Bach creates feminine clothing with subtle tomboy undertones. With slip dresses, knitwear, gowns, and simple jersey pieces featured throughout her collections, the designer offers both wardrobe essentials and red carpet showpieces.

Recent collections feature delicate floral embroidery, ruffles, pleats, and fluid forms. Her experimentation with a range of different fabrics and clean color palettes makes for a diverse and very wearable collection.

Accessories and footwear are also key to the designer's collections; for Spring/Summer 2016 and previous seasons, Malene has collaborated with Gold Dot to create bold and edgy platform heels. In addition, sunglasses and leather goods are incorporated.

Malene has evolved since being handpicked and awarded "Ones to Watch"; she has acquired a loyal industry fanbase on her professional journey and has been featured in *Vogue*, *ELLE*, *Marie Claire*, and *Grazia*.

The brand also boasts a series of celebrity wearers including Claudia Schiffer, Natalie Dormer, Diana Agron, and Eleanor Thomlinson.

The clothes adopt a modern approach to the feminine form and present it in a beautifully crafted way.

How do you start the research process?
Our research processes tend to start with the textiles, as these take center stage in all of our collections. We explore a narrowed-down selection of fabrics from our mills and then redevelop these in various ways; color ways, composition, etc., until we are happy with the outcome.

The textiles then inform the research. At times there's limitations on how the fabrics can be used, so obviously this needs to be carefully considered during the research and design processes.

We work from mood images that create an overall mood for the collection, but the main research is spent on exploring shapes, design details, and textures all generated from looking at a large spectrum varying from vintage clothing, previous seasons, to working on the stand. Everything has been done before. A shirt is a shirt at the end of the day. The design process is all about adding your signature to the designs to make them "yours" and by that differ from what has been done in the past.

What are your sources of inspiration?
Everyday life. Whether it's looking at people's clothing on public transport to nature surrounding you, when walking the dog in the park. Also, the past is always a source of inspiration. Rummaging in charity and vintage shops and looking for design details and textures that can then be altered, collated, and brought up-to-date to sit within the collections.

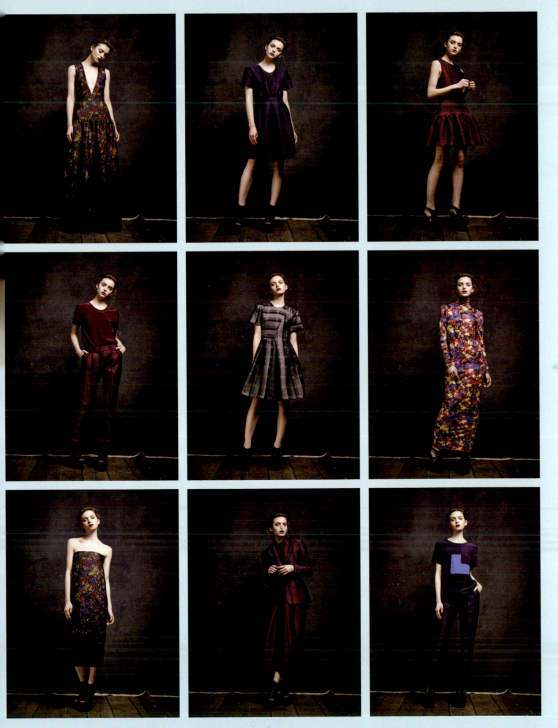

Images of Malene Oddershede Bach's Autumn/Winter 2015–16 collection.

Do you set themes? If so, how and where do you work?

Not as such. We do set ourselves more of an overall feeling for the collection. The main themes, if any, would be the textiles and various design details that are then developed in a variety of forms throughout the collections.

What kind of brief/constraints/direction/market do you work to?

Our collections have been changing over the last few seasons according to the market. It's important to understand the market and bear in mind demands. At the same time, however, it's important not to allow the market to give you too many constraints, as this can have a knock-on effect on the creativity within the collections. Saying that, our direction is very much to create high-end ready-to-wear clothing, which is both wearable and commercial.

We don't work towards a specific market as such. More towards a specific woman. It's important to understand who your customers are.

Do you have sources that you repeat or revisit in seasons or collections?

It's important to keep certain signatures within the collections, so the collection is recognizable and so as not to alienate your buyers and customers. This often results in reworking certain design details used in the past and which we use to initially inform design details within the new collections.

Do you have a signature style?

While our collections are continuously developing and changing as the brand grows, we still work with the same aesthetics, and consequently, the brand signatures remain within the collection, but perhaps with an ever so slightly different appearance.

How important is the research to the design process?

The research process is always important, as this will inform the overall collection and also ensure that this is coherent throughout.

How do you collate your research?

We have these massive cork walls in our studio, which grow and develop continuously throughout the research project from initial fabric ideas; to textures, drawings, design developments in the form of samples, etc., and eventually it's narrowed down, only focusing on actual elements residing within the collection, and the collection designs are created alongside it.

After every season the wall is cleared and the process starts all over again. The journey one has traveled from beginning to end, developing a collection from ideas to reality is truly fascinating.

What advice would you give to anyone interested in a career in fashion/fashion forecasting?

Make sure to get as much work experience in the industry while studying, as these experiences are what will form you, not just as a student but also later in life as a professional within the fashion industry. Moreover, the contacts created throughout this time are vital, as these are what you will build upon later in your career.

Be true to yourself. While the industry might look glamorous from the outside, it's far from reality. Working as a creative within the fashion industry is hard work and involves long working hours. Creativity is all about enjoying what you are doing. If you are not prepared to put the work in, then it might not be the right career path.

Image of Malene Oddershede Bach's Autumn/Winter 2015–16 collection.

Interview

Paul Rawson

In 2007 Paul graduated from the MA Womenswear course at Central Saint Martins College of Art and Design. He has worked as a pattern cutter for a number of designers, including Alexander McQueen and Giles. For the last seven years, he has been Assistant to Stevie Stewart (formerly of Bodymap), working on a range of projects, developing and producing costumes and outfits for contemporary dance companies such as Michael Clark Company, Russell Maliphant, and Ballet Rambert. He has also produced outfits for a number of music tours and music videos for artists such as Kylie Minogue, Britney Spears, and Cheryl Cole.

Paul joined Middlesex University in 2012 and is currently Program Leader for BA (Hons) Fashion Design. Previously, he worked as a Senior Lecturer at De Montfort University and taught other Fashion Design courses at UCA Epsom, Central Saint Martins, and Northampton University.

The Fashion Design Program at Middlesex University creates talented, dynamic, and creative designers who are ready to face the challenges of the industry. The degree represents the best of London's emerging talent, with designers excelling in both skill and imagination. The team pride themselves on their strong menswear and innovative womenswear, demonstrating the perfect balance between design, cut, and textiles.

As a fashion educator, what is your approach to research within the design process and what importance do you give it?

Research can take many forms from moving image to text, essentially something that creates a reaction and provokes a response with the individual exploring it. It is the most important part of the design process. Before any real design work can begin, initial research must be carried out, responded to, evaluated, and edited. This could be collecting images, watching film, visiting exhibitions, observing people. Most importantly, it must be explored in depth; there should be a hunger to find out everything possible surrounding the subject. It is an ongoing process, some elements or images will be of huge importance, some references will be filed for later, and others will be discarded altogether. This process of researching, sourcing, and editing should continue throughout the development of any design project to help solve problems and fully resolve ideas.

What does research mean to you? How do you encourage students to present their research?

For me, research is the foundation of any design project, firstly taking the form of visuals, concept imagery, and ideas for silhouette, color, details, and fabrication. These visuals could be anything from famous works of art to a picture of a coffee stain, but most importantly must mean something to the individual using them. Secondly, fabrication, trims, fastenings, etc.—all of these elements form basic research. It is also sampling of these details, finishes, and any techniques to resolve and develop personal responses and individual ideas.

At Middlesex we encourage our students to present their research in a way that reflects them as a designer. It is important to me that we do not create a "house style" through presentation, so individuality is extremely important. Documenting a thought process is also something I place huge importance on; it is essential that research visuals be accompanied by responses, whether that be design drawings, sketches, fabrics, or details. Each image should be of importance, carefully selected, and edited.

What changes have you seen in the education of fashion over the years (try to be positive!)?

Over the years I have seen a change in the range of courses available to students. The development of more diverse programs to allow students to really focus on which area of the fashion industry they would like a career in is really positive.

There has also been a change in the way students research; the Internet makes everything instantly accessible, which has its positives in instantly accessing everything, but can also lead to lazy research and poor quality images. More importantly, I think it can ruin the experience of research. While looking through books and magazines in a library, for instance, you often stumble over an inspiring image that might not exist online or wasn't linked to the search you entered; or the sensation of going to a gallery to really experience the scale, color, or depth of a piece of art or visiting an archive to actually touch and look inside historical or iconic pieces of fashion—all of these things enrich the research process and ultimately the work produced.

What is the (design) philosophy of the BA Fashion Design at Middlesex University?

At Middlesex we promote individuality. Looking at our shows, you will see that not one collection is in any way the same as another. Our portfolios are diverse in content, illustration style, and presentation. It is important to us that students are able to research and develop collections that are true to themselves, inspired by their own interests, and carrying their own individual identity.

Our students are taught the traditional rules of cutting and manufacture and are then encouraged to question them, often producing innovative silhouette, detailing, fabrication, and finishes. We encourage our students to develop their own textiles, techniques, and fabrics to enable extremely individual design projects and collections throughout their three years of study with us. The great facilities we have at Middlesex University allow us to cross-fertilize between various design departments and disciplines, promoting transfer of knowledge and replicating industry practice.

Ultimately, our job as fashion educators is to guide, nurture, and challenge our students to produce their best possible work and ultimately produce the next generation of autonomous designers, researchers, cutters, and makers that are ready for a lifelong career in this exciting industry.

When you look at student application portfolios, what do you look for?
There are three specific things I look for in an application portfolio. The first is evidence of personal creativity; this could take any form. It could be fashion, but it could equally be sculpture or photography or something that the student has created themselves. The second is an ability to draw, whether that is fashion drawing, illustrations, or some life drawing. It may also be beneficial if there were observations of real clothing, allowing understanding of actual garments.

The third thing is the most important, and that is documentation of the thought process. So how that amazing image has been used to inform the outcome, this can take the form of sketches, samples, and annotation but should be rich and predominantly visual. This is the thing that makes each student different—the way that they think. Everything else we can teach!

What in your opinion makes a successful fashion student?
I believe a successful fashion student has to work hard, have a passion and belief in what they are doing; they should be absorbing culture and everything around them constantly and using it to inform their design choices. They should have an opinion on everything and a reason for it; if they love something, then why? They should be open to challenge, having all areas of their work questioned, criticized, as well as praised.

There should always be a hunger for more, to know more, to experience more, to do more!

What does a newly graduated designer need to consider on entering the workplace?
Primarily, graduates should consider that they are entering a different kind of learning experience; they should continue to absorb everything around them in the same way they did in university education. They should be prepared and willing to do anything asked of them and treat it as experience. Ultimately, try to be indispensable and leave your ego at home!

What advice would you give to anyone interested in a career in fashion? And what advice would you give to a fashion graduate?
Firstly, really consider what area of fashion you are interested in; the industry is huge and there are many diverse roles within it, so identifying your specific area of interest will help define your choices, focus your work, and achieve your goals.

Understand that it is extremely competitive; there is always someone willing to do what you can do better, or for less.

Realize that this is an industry; it takes a lot of hard work, ambition, and commitment to succeed within it. Contrary to belief, it is not all champagne, shopping, and parties!

Images of outfits from the final year BA (Hons) Fashion Design 2015.

Choosing what to research

Now that you have a good understanding of what research is and what it needs to contain in order to be useful and relevant, you need to find out where to obtain this information.

In this chapter, we explain how to go about choosing a concept and setting a theme—whether abstract, conceptual, or narrative. We also explain the differences between primary and secondary sources, because using both in your research will be essential. We also explore the different sources of inspiration available, from museums and art galleries to the natural world and architecture.

Womenswear from Christopher Raeburn's Spring/Summer 2016 collection "Sarawak."

"Fashion is not something that exists in dresses only. Fashion is in the sky, in the street, fashion has to do with ideas, the way we live, what is happening."
Coco Chanel

Choosing a theme

When it comes to choosing a theme for your collection, you first need to consider how it responds to the brief (if there is one), and second, you need to ensure that it will inspire you to be creative. You may have already explored words and images in the brainstorming process (pages 22–23), and they will therefore assist in the collation of ideas into a possible theme or concept.

A theme or concept is the essence of a good collection and is what makes it unique and personal to you. Remember: Good designers will explore aspects of their own personality, interests and viewpoints about the world around them, fusing them into a vibrant, innovative, and credible collection. A theme may be driven by several different approaches, as explored in the following pages.

Visual inspiration

In an abstract, you might explore a variety of unrelated visual sources that can be drawn together because of similar or juxtaposed qualities. For example, you might consider a photograph of a piece of mineral rock and a shell, alongside a piece of pleated fabric and images of the artists Christo and Jeanne-Claude's installation work, such as their wrapping of the Reichstag Building in Berlin, Germany, with fabric. This combination of information might also possess similar qualities that you could explore, translating into shapes, textures, and colors in the design of your collection.

Conceptual inspiration

Using a concept is when you work with a word, description, or methodology—for example, *surrealism*. You then translate it into a series of ideas, or it directs your approach to the research and design. Think: what images and words would you associate with surrealism? How might a garment eventually express this word or concept?

Research boards exploring various themes.

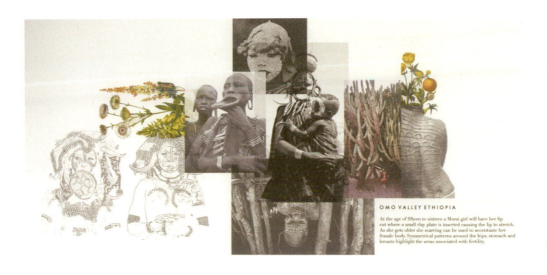

OMO VALLEY ETHIOPIA

At the age of fifteen to sixteen a Mursi girl will have her lip cut where a small clay plate is inserted causing the lip to stretch. As she gets older she scarring can be used to accentuate her female body. Symmetrical patterns around the hips, stomach and breasts highlight the areas associated with fertility.

Narrative inspiration

Narrative, by its definition, means a written account of something, perhaps a story or a tale.

Designer John Galliano is famous for creating stories and characters for his collections, often creating a muse as his central focus; for example, the 1920s' dancer Josephine Baker was the inspiration in one collection, as was the Countess de Castiglione in another. Each of these characters brings style and also a personality to bear on the process; it also helps to direct the sources of research and design, as well as the final presentation of the collection.

It is important to remember that regardless of how you start the generation of ideas, the world's fashion buyers and press will ultimately judge you on the clothes.

Research board drawing inspiration from African tribal culture.

> "It's great to tell a story in a collection, but you must never forget that, despite all the fantasy, the thing is about clothes."
> John Galliano
> (Galliano, Colin McDowell, Weidenfeld & Nicolson)

What are primary sources?

Primary sources are the findings that you have collected or recorded firsthand. In other words, they are the objects that you have drawn directly from—for example, anatomical references from a museum of natural history. When you see a painting "in the flesh," it is very different from seeing it in a book or online in terms of scale, texture, detail, and presence.

Tropical fish or coral seen online or in a book will never compare with seeing them in nature or in an aquarium.

Primary sources are generally recorded through drawings or photographs, and often provide greater sensory associations than just the object itself. For example, touch and smell may all recall memories and be included in the design process.

Examples from student sketchbooks of primary research using photography.

A natural spectacle
Specimens of plants and insects.

Human skulls & natural history and diseases of the teeth

Old Operating Theatre Museum

What are secondary sources?

Secondary sources are the findings of other people. These may be found in books, on the Internet, or in journals and magazines. They are just as important as primary sources of research and often allow you to see and read about things that are no longer available or that are not easily accessible. It is vital that you understand both types of sources and that in any good research there is a balance of both. Primary sources call upon your drawing talents, and secondary sources utilize your investigative skills, so be prepared to bring both together in your design research.

Jewels of the Lodge of Antiquity No 2

32 nd Degree Collar,Ancient and Accepted Rite

REGALIA of the late Bro Maurice Vidal Portman, 33rd Degree

FINCH DIAGRAM, published in May 1810

Sources of inspiration

You should now understand what research is and the elements it should contain in order for you to design from it. We have also explored the need for a concept or theme (see pages 34–35). So where do you find the information you need to begin the process of gathering your research? Where do you go for sources of inspiration?

Online fashion resources

The Internet is often the easiest and the first place to start research, as it is the most accessible way of gathering information, images, and text from all over the world. Using search engines to find websites dedicated to the subject you have begun to look at is often the fastest way to find inspiration. However, the information found online can often be limited in scope and unreferenced, so it is never a substitute for primary research or secondary research that takes place in the real world.

Remember that research is not just about visual inspiration; it is also about tangible, practical things, such as fabric sourcing. The Internet allows you to get in touch with companies and manufacturers who may be able to provide you with fabric samples, trimmings, and specialist skills in production or finishing.

Take a look at specialist online fashion-related resources, such as costume archives, manufacturing and fabric wholesalers, specific trend and forecasting companies, and industry events such as Premier Vision, which showcases the latest fabrics from around the world. Having a good "fashion awareness" is essential if you are to progress within the industry.

Fashion blogs

Blogs are a saturated area of the fashion media industry. Within the global community that we all now live in, fashion blogs enable people to review, discuss, and follow styles and trends from all around the world. In terms of research value, blogs offer an opportunity for you to gather style and trend information very easily and apply this to market awareness and new product development.

Fashion blogs can be categorized into many different fields, such as street style, high-street fashion, haute couture, shoes, handbags, eco-fashion, and celebrity style, for instance.

Increasingly people are using sites such as Tumblr, Instagram, and Pinterest to share their creative output and to connect with other like-minded creative people. Video-sharing platforms such as Vimeo and YouTube allow video bloggers to share opinions and information that might provoke a line of inquiry in your research or enable you to assess how someone else thinks.

Fashion blogs are a vital part of the mainstream fashion media and can be easily accessed by a huge and diverse market. Blogs are also now integral to the PR strategies of many large fashion companies, as they provide an opportunity for companies to promote their products and simultaneously enable interactive communication with their customers.

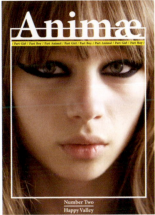

Animæ magazine issues 1, 2, and 3.

Anyone can write a blog, but in general blogs fall into three distinct categories, in terms of whether they are written by insiders, outsiders, or aspiring insiders:

- Insiders are those who work in the fashion industry and are able to offer professional opinions and points of view on current trends or products.

- Outsiders are those people who don't work within the fashion industry but have a strong opinion on fashion due to their personal interest in it as a consumer.

- Finally, aspiring insiders are those people who wish to work in the industry and see blogging as a new media and a means of gaining attention and possible employment. Many of these aspiring insiders have indeed found employment and are often invited to feature on mainstream media websites and to comment on events such as fashion weeks and individual designer shows.

Magazines

Knowing your subject and having an awareness of fashion are essential to the research process, and magazines are a good place to develop this knowledge.

Magazines are a great source of information and potential inspiration for the designer. They can provide you with images of the latest trends, styles, and garments from other designers in the industry. They also give you insight into other aspects you should consider as a designer— for example, lifestyle and cultural interests that may affect the market you wish to design for. They can be visually stimulating and a great resource for beginning to identify key stylists, photographers, make-up artists, and hair stylists from the fashion industry.

"As the boundaries between blogs, online magazines and media platforms continues to blur, there has been a huge international resurgence in the popularity of print media due to the reduced cost of digital publishing and partly as a reaction to the vast amount of digital information available.

Nearly all new and established fashion magazine titles will have a digital presence or online platform to complement their print offering. Social media is also a key component in disseminating up to the minute information, sharing inspiration and allows the audience to join in the conversation."
Matt Ryalls, editor and art director at *Animœ* magazine

Online magazines

Online magazines also allow for mixed media presentations of information. So in addition to written content, they can show visuals not only through photographs but also through video and film footage, such as the latest catwalk shows or designer interviews.

Because the cost of setting up an online magazine is relatively low, far more diverse and niche market sites are set up to cater for specific consumers and markets of fashion. Such areas of interest, for instance, may feature the latest collections and up-to-the-minute fashion news, lifestyle, trends, retail information, industry and manufacturing, global street life, and youth subculture genres.

Online magazines allow you to review and research the most current information as well as access new and up-and-coming creatives, designers, stylists, photographers, and writers from around the world. Access to this wealth of information and insight into the industry is vital to any well-informed designer and should play a major part of any design student's good practice when it comes to researching a new product or idea. Knowing your subject is vital to the success of any design project or brief. Fashion, by its very definition, is about current styles and trends, so online magazines are more able to quickly update and refresh new and changing information about current styles and ideas.

Libraries, books, and journals

A library is a wonderful place to begin your research, as it can offer immediate references for images and text in the form of books and journals. A library allows you to explore aisles of books on subjects that you may not have initially considered during your brainstorming sessions. There is something special about leafing through a book; the smell, touch, and visual stimulus they can provide are often forgotten when simply looking on the Internet. Books are things that are themselves crafted and designed. Viewing an original manuscript of Victorian drawings is far more inspirational than seeing them on a computer screen.

You should be able to access a library in almost every town and city, and it can provide you with a general and broad selection of books. However, if you are studying at a college or university, you should have access to a much more specific range of books and journals that will be more usefully related to your interests and the courses taught there.

Museums and art galleries

Museums are an excellent source of primary research, as they contain a huge and diverse array of objects, artifacts, and historical treasures. Often museums are dedicated to specific interests, such as the military, science, natural history, or the arts.

Places such as the Victoria and Albert Museum in London or the Metropolitan Museum of Art in New York are vast palaces of global art, design, history, and culture. They offer the designer a great starting point to the research process, enabling you to explore many galleries and rooms dedicated to different subjects, countries, and periods. The possibilities are under one roof but have the potential to be endless.

Art galleries are also an essential part of the research process, as they offer inspiration for subject matter, color, texture, print, and surface embellishment.

Artists have directly influenced many collections by fashion designers. For example, Versace used Andy Warhol's Marilyn Monroe pop art print from the 1960s as the inspiration for a print on a dress, Yves Saint Laurent incorporated Mondrian's graphic work onto a shift dress during the 1960s, and Elsa Schiaparelli worked with the surrealist artist Salvador Dali on many pieces during the 1930s.

Paintings can also provide you with a picture of life and dress from a period or country where photography was not present—for example, Renaissance art and sculpture in Rome or perhaps scriptures from Egyptian times. Most towns and cities have a central museum and art gallery, so it is wise to explore what is available because you may find hidden treasures worth further investigation.

Model wearing a "Mondrian dress" walks the runway during Yves Saint Laurent Spring/Summer 2002 haute couture collections.

Costume

As a fashion designer, you need to have a reasonable working knowledge of dress/costume history. Understanding what has been done in the past allows you to expand from this and take it into the future. Taking inspiration from period dress allows you to exploit old styles of shape, construction, fit, print, and embroidery and develop new interpretations of them. With such a rich and diverse dress history available, you can develop many references into your collection. Designers and design labels like Alexander McQueen, Vivienne Westwood, and John Galliano are famous for utilizing costume influences in their collections. Places like the Victoria and Albert Museum in London and the Fashion Museum in Bath, UK, contain wonderful collections of period dress that you can access and draw from in your research. There are also private archives, such as the ones owned by the London College of Fashion and another by the Fashion Institute in New York, that you can access; parts of them are often on display in the galleries. Some local museums contain small collections of dress history that often give insight into the people of that town or city. You also can find or purchase costume or vintage clothing if you know where to look.

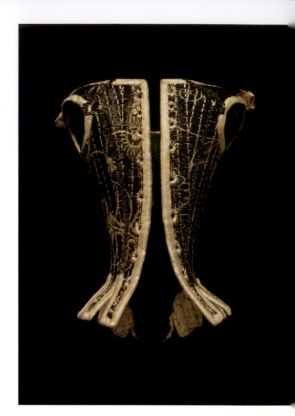

A corset for a doll by Lady Clapham Doll's clothes. Silver and silk. Britain, c. 1690.

Coat, by Emile Pingat (1820–1901). Ivory silk with feather motif and white fur around collar. France, 1885.

Travel

When you are a designer, it is important to explore and discover your environment and realize that everything around you has the potential to be research. Therefore, the ability to travel can also be an important part of the research process. Looking at and learning from other cultures and countries can provide you with a wealth of information that can be translated into contemporary fashion design.

Large design companies often send their design teams abroad to research for their collections, with the intent to gather books, pieces of fabric or trims, artifacts, garments, jewelry, and accessories—anything they think could be used as inspiration. Photographs and drawings are a vital part of recording your experiences of traveling to another country. As an aspiring designer, you should consider that a holiday abroad can also be an opportunity to gather research.

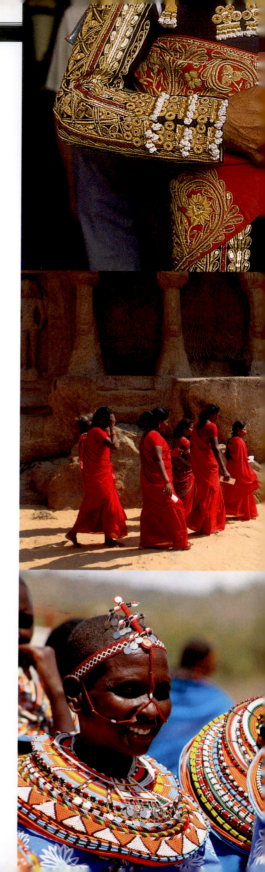

Inspiration board showing examples of world costume and dress.

> **"The novelties of one generation are only the resuscitated fashions of the generation before last."**
> George Bernard Shaw

Flea markets and vintage stores

We have already discussed that research is about poking and prying, sourcing information, and always being on the lookout for references for design. Flea markets, vintage stores, and charity shops/thrift stores offer you an ideal opportunity to discover old treasures, discarded artifacts, and vintage or period clothes by simply wandering in and around them. Most of the great fashion capitals of the world have good areas to search for such markets and shops; for example, Portobello Road Market in London, Greenwich Village in New York, and Montmartre in Paris. Some designers have built their individual design identity on using vintage or recycled components in their collections.

The famous Portobello Road Market in London is a treasure trove of vintage and antique finds.

Exercise 2

Using primary and secondary research sources

For this exercise you will practice using both primary and secondary sources of research and their relationship to each other.

As discussed in this chapter, primary sources are the findings that you have collected or recorded firsthand. Primary research can be gathered from many sources, such as museums and art galleries, flea markets, and specialist shops.

Primary research can be recorded through drawings and photographs. You may even write about the experience, such as what emotions (if any) you experienced when seeing the object firsthand. For instance, art can inspire intense feelings, and perhaps these can be harnessed as part of your research experience.

Secondary sources are the findings of other people. They may be found in books, on the Internet, or in journals and magazines. They are just as important as primary sources of research and often allow you to see and read about things that are no longer available or that are not easily accessible.

Secondary research is investigative and requires you to be curious about a subject. Secondary research can also be recorded through drawings and photographs, as well as photocopies, printouts, scans, and tear sheets from magazines.

Primary sources call upon your drawing talents, and secondary sources utilize your investigative skills. Both types of sources are essential to the research process. Either can come first: a book you are curious about might provide a starting point for your research that you then develop by visiting firsthand relevant places to find examples of things "in the flesh." Likewise, a visit to an art gallery might inspire you to delve deeper into the work of a particular artist or designer, and this might take place by looking through books or on the Internet. However, for this exercise, it is perhaps easier to start with primary sources.

Investigate what local resources are available to you in terms of museums, galleries, or specialist shops. Visit these places; you may visit more than one before you decide on the direction of your research. Record things of interest through drawings and photographs.

Now choose the elements from your visits that you find the most inspiring and develop them exploring secondary sources. This will give your initial (primary) research much more depth. Explore any avenues of research that you think might be relevant and do not skimp on the quantity! One or two images do not constitute in-depth research!

Architecture

Fashion and architecture have a great deal in common; they start from the same point—the human body. They both protect and shelter, while also providing a means to express identity, whether it is personal, political, religious, or cultural.

Fashion and architecture also express ideas of space, volume, and movement and have parallel practices in the way that they exploit materials from flat two-dimensional surfaces to complex three-dimensional forms. Because of this common factor, architecture is a great subject matter to use in research as a fashion designer.

Like costume, architecture can express period trends and has often linked itself with social interests, as well as changes in technology, in particular the use of new materials and production techniques.

You only need to look at the work of the Spanish architect Gaudi in the late 1800s and early 1900s and his interest in the natural world, and the related art and dress movement his work was part of, to see how closely fashion and architecture are linked.

More recently, Japanese designers such as Yohji Yamamoto and Comme des Garçons have demonstrated clear similarities in the garments that they create and the contemporary architecture that they are surrounded by.

Clear visual and structural links can be made between these Balmain dresses (Spring/Summer 2015) and architecture. For example, this building from the Golden Lane Housing Estate in London, built by the architects Chamberlin, Powell, and Bon in 1982.

"Fashion is architecture.
It is a matter of proportions."
Coco Chanel

The natural world

The natural world provides a vast and diverse source of inspiration for gathering primary information. It is a source of visual stimuli that can inspire all of the key elements you need to determine in your research, such as shapes, structures, colors, patterns, and textures. Your interest may lead you to look at rare birds of paradise or butterflies and insects. It may be that you explore the patterns of snakes or the jungle foliage of a rainforest. The opportunities are endless—and as a source of inspiration, the natural world is one that designers constantly explore.

Alexander McQueen; Savage Beauty V&A Museum 2015.

Chanel haute couture Spring/Summer 2015.

Iris Van Herpen haute couture Autumn/Winter 2011/12.

Film, theater, and music

The film, theater, and music industries have always had very close links to fashion. The famous Hollywood starlets of the 1930s and '40s were always photographed dressed in garments by French designers such as Lanvin, Balenciaga, and Dior. The glamorous, unattainable lives they led only added to the allure of the clothes that they wore, spurring on designers to create even more fantastic pieces.

In more recent times, rock and pop stars have tended to excite and create a lifestyle that people want to aspire to. Through associations with designers and brands, they often promote collections in videos, promos, movies, and publications. Vivienne Westwood and Malcolm McLaren, for instance, famously dressed the Sex Pistols in the 1970s and started a whole new subcultural movement called punk.

Today the links between music and fashion are so close that we are now in an era when big hip-hop and rap stars, such as Jay Z and Kanye West, routinely create their own fashion labels and promote them through music.

Meanwhile, former pop star Victoria Beckham has readily made the transition from fashion muse to fashion designer, having shown credible collections at New York Fashion Week and opening her first stand-alone store in London.

Due to such close associations between the music and film industries, these are certainly areas that you may wish to explore as sources of inspiration— whether it be to start your collection with a muse or by looking to a movie theme as a possible direction to research more fully.

An outfit by Marc Jacobs, Spring/Summer 2016, making direct reference to film.

Street and youth culture

We have already looked at the importance of contemporary trends and how these are often related to global and cultural interests and changes in taste. And we have referred to the "bubble-up effect"— how trends can form on the street and influence catwalk designs and ultimately what is fashionable in the mainstream.

It is therefore essential that the research process should include possible inspiration from the street and from subcultures or special interest groups. Influences may come from trends in clothing styles—for example, grunge, the Harajuku girls from Tokyo, the skateboarders from Downtown LA, or the club kids from the 1990s in New York.

All of these subculture youth groups have an identity and style of their own and have influenced many designers' collections in the past, from the clothes to the make-up and styling. By looking to and experiencing street culture and what it has to offer at any one moment, in any one city, you can filter out trends and interests and identify what is fresh, new, and directional. Street culture can also be an area to look back on as old street styles have also influenced contemporary designers.

Some images of original punk subculture of the late 1970s/early 1980s.

Punk inspired outfit by Hedi Slimane for Saint Laurent, Autumn/Winter 2015.

New technologies

The development of new technologies in the fashion industry has always played a role in the design and research process.

During the 1960s, a huge technological breakthrough in synthetic fibers and an interest in space and the future inspired a generation of young designers, such as Mary Quant, André Courrèges, and Pierre Cardin.

More recently, there have been significant technological developments in digital printing. Designers such as Mary Katrantzou and Peter Pilotto have made full use of these new techniques in their signature prints for their collections. Designers such as Hussein Chalayan and Iris van Herpen also construct their garments out of a whole new generation of fabrics and materials. E-textiles (or "smart textiles") enable computing and digital components to become embedded into everyday garments as "wearable technology," and these are developing quickly, matching technological innovation with fashion.

As a designer, you need to be aware of new technologies and developments—as well as future ones—and how they might inform or impact on your work as a fashion designer.

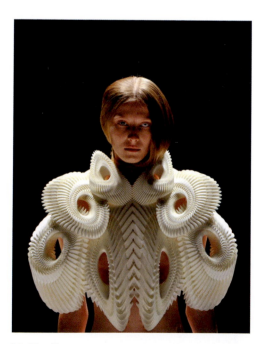

Iris Van Herpen,
Spring/Summer 2012.

Iris Van Herpen haute couture,
Autumn/Winter 2011–12.

Forecasting and trend agencies

Forecasting and trend agencies can also be a possible source of inspiration.

As already discussed, having an awareness of street cultures, new trends, new technologies, and global interests is important when it comes to researching for a new collection or the development of a new brand.

Tracking trends is not just about looking at fashion, but also about looking at demographics, behavior, technologies, and lifestyle. Consumer analysis will often help a designer create the right clothes and accessories for people in the future.

Companies will spend huge amounts of their budgets to gain this sort of insight into the market and what they then need to focus their ideas toward.

Fashion forecasting agencies are companies set up to support the industry and specifically look at current trends and cultural pursuits. They are, through market research, able to offer the designer a glimpse into ideas and directions that are becoming popular in society. These ideas can take the form of colors, fabrics, details, and shapes, all of which are essential to the creative process as a fashion designer.

The information these agencies produce can be accessed through specialist magazines and trend books, as well as through presentations at trade fairs such as Premier Vision in Paris.

Read the full interview with the trend forecasting agency WGSN on pages 138–139.

Exercise 3
Trends

Trends can be localized or global, starting on the street or filtering down from high fashion. Trends can be analyzed and predicted, but they can also be coincidences. Designers operating in a fashion capital are experiencing the same cultural and social factors as each other; seeing the same exhibitions, seeing the same films, drinking in the same cafés and bars, visiting the same markets and shops. So it is hardly surprising that some similarities or trends might occur in the fashion collections they produced.

This exercise is in two parts; the first part is about people watching. Find a busy spot in your neighborhood (a café with an outdoor space is ideal); sit down and record what passersby are wearing by drawing or photographing them (you might want to be discreet). You might feel bold and ask people directly if you can take their photograph for a project. After you have recorded enough people, take an overview of everyone and see if you can spot any trends in the way that people dress.

The second part is to look at the most recent fashion collections online (ready-to-wear collections are probably the best for this exercise; look at vogue. com, style.com, etc.). Look at as many collections from each city as possible and then see whether you can identify any trends that can be seen in the collections of one fashion capital. Then compare the collections of one city with another and, again, see if you can spot any trends.

Sustainability and ethics

Fashion makes an important contribution to society. It creates jobs and products that satisfy fundamental human needs. Yet it can also damage individuals and societies more widely through poor working practices, and the detrimental psychological and ecological effects of consumerist fashion. A fashion piece cannot in itself create sustainability; this is created by the process in which we design, make, wear, discard, and reincarnate it. We need to design in a way that means we engage in fashion in a sustainable manner.

In a society obsessed with instant gratification and conspicuous consumption (or "fast fashion"), it's easy to dismiss fashion design as frivolous. Skirt lengths and denim washes appear inconsequential when juxtaposed with real-world concerns like climate change, economic strife, water shortages, hunger, and malnutrition. But if you consider the fact that clothing is something we envelop our bodies with every single day, to ignore the apparel industry's environmental and social impact would be simply negligent.

Changing fashion practices to improve the well-being of workers, consumers, designers, and producers is central to a more sustainable future. The impact of the fashion sector on natural resources and ecosystems is substantial. There is an urgent need to reduce the negative effects of producing and consuming fashion. The use of organic clothing, produced without toxic pesticides and dipped in low-impact dyes, is just one of the ways in which we, as designers, can start to change the very real impact that fashion has on the global environment.

Sustainability is an essential consideration when designing. Not only will it make you more aware of current trends within this movement, but it will also give you the edge when leaving education and entering the industry. Be inspired to think about and act on what you can do to make a difference in fashion and textiles, and how you can contribute toward building a sustainable future.

Christopher Raeburn is a designer deeply concerned with the sustainability of his designs. These images are from his Spring/Summer 2016 collection.

Recycled garment manipulation

With flea markets, charity shops, and vintage stores providing such a wealth of material and inspiration, it is important to consider how this tangible inspiration can be used for potential design direction. It is not simply about looking at and learning from the objects and garments found; it can also be about how they can be manipulated, draped, and deconstructed to discover new and hidden directions. Furthermore, the use of recycling is not only an inventive way of researching and developing design ideas, but is also one that has a sustainable and ethical consideration. Working with recycled garments through draping, disassembling, and deconstructing them can provide you with many new and inventive ideas, and is a great way to start analyzing and interpreting your research. By taking garments apart, you can also start to learn about how they were constructed and even begin to understand basic flat pattern development.

The deconstruction of recycled garments is a great way to begin to push against the traditional constraints of fashion. Exploring proportion and scale, placement and displacement, symmetry and asymmetry, as well as the juxtaposition of fabrics, textures, prints, and garment types is a great way to get you thinking and developing early ideas for garments and design possibilities.

What happens when you take a traditional men's trench coat and take apart the different components, such as the collar, sleeves, storm flaps, and belt, and blend and drape them onto a ladies' jersey dress or even a classic men's shirt? The hybrid garment becomes new and exciting and offers up avenues for further exploration and design. It is important that you record all of your experimentation either through photography or drawing, as these three-dimensional experiments will provide you with further research and analysis to work from in the designs later on.

A skirt showing recycled garment manipulation.

Exercise 4
Recycled garment manipulation

In this exercise, you will explore and record three-dimensional recycled garment manipulation and deconstruction techniques. You will need to source a range of second-hand garments from a charity shop or flea market. It is best if you can gather several different types of garments in different fabrics and perhaps even look for nongarment items to drape, such as tablecloths and shawls.

You will need access to a mannequin or dress stand, either full-scale or half-scale, as well as pins, scissors, quick-stitch unpick, a camera, and drawing media.

Look at each of the items you have found. Place them in their usual form on the dress stand. Make a drawing and/or take a photograph. Analyze and record the different components that make up the garment, such as seams, panels, collars, cuffs, and sleeves, and details such as pockets, belts, epaulettes, buttons, lapels, storm flaps, pleats, and linings.

Now that you have fully explored and examined the garment as it is, it is time to model and drape with the garment from different viewpoints. So, first turn the garment upside down. If it has sleeves or legs, what happens when they are used for a different purpose or are connected? Can a collar become a hemline detail? Can you turn a sleeve inside out to form a pocket? Reposition the center front to the center back, or even create a side-seam opening perhaps.

Now take another garment from your stock and quickly unpick it or simply cut it open at the seams. Disassemble the components, such as the sleeves, collars, cuffs, waistbands, pockets, and linings. Now start to pin and model these onto the other garment; consider both regular and irregular placement. Work with different combinations of garments, such as a dress and a coat, or a shirt and trousers. How do the different pieces start to work against and with one another?

As you explore a range of combinations, make sure that you record each of them using either your camera or through drawing. Record the garments from all sides, as details and silhouettes could be created on all 360 degrees of the stand.

Suggested items could be some from the following list:

- men's large cotton shirts
- T-shirts or jersey items
- a man's (or a woman's) suit jacket and trousers
- trench coat
- ladies' printed dresses
- denim jackets and jeans
- old leather coat
- lace trims or table cloths
- accessories such as belts, large or decorative bags, shawls, stoles, and furs (depending on your views)

Interview
Dr. Noki

Dr. Noki studied at Edinburgh School of Art. Before setting up his own label, he worked with Helen Storey, Whitaker Malem, and Owen Gastor, from whom he learned "eco-thinking, arts and crafts, and futuristic thinking," respectively. Noki is a subversive artist/designer, customizer, and stylist based in the East End of London, having been dragged up in the Old Street/Shoreditch areas circa 1995. He is famously anonymous, recognizable only by the "SOB" (Suffocation Of Branding) masks that he wears.

Noki is an anagram and pun, a playful subversion on the IKONic globalized fashion brand. Noki experiments with customization by collaging the "sustainable canvas" together with creative cutting, stitching, appliqué, and silk-screen printing, thereby creating a new genre of street couture.

How did you get started with the whole idea of using rags or recycled garments as a way of designing?
As a textile artist I don't feel I'm designing at all; it's all one big collage and sculptural exercise to me. I need the "rejected designed garment" to start my creative process through customizing techniques I've developed over the past 20 years.

It all started around 1995. I had left Edinburgh Art College and arrived in London and found a warehouse in Leonard Street in Shoreditch. It was a total ghost town.

I've always been a brand obsessive, wearing them with pride, and coming from the rave generation of 1988 at the age of 16, sportswear was our tribal uniform. Its look was totally alien to the tribes beforehand, our music was NEW, electronic based and generated a different driven sweaty emotion. Sportswear and trainers provided the comfortable style every new generation craved. With sportswear, big corporate bill boarding is inevitable. I'd just got to a stage in my life when I desired to change my perspective and subvert its message yet keep a love for its function and design perfection. So I started chopping up sportswear, collaging its technical details together in a new configuration and Noki was born.

Examples of work by Dr. Noki.

Do you have a political statement to make with your work?

I first started making big textile magazines by sewing two T-shirts together. This was my art statement to my generation; we believed more in the printed words on garments than in books. So like the DADA art movement that always intrigued me, I found my alphabet from brand identity. So I suppose there is a political agenda of sorts that involves looking further, always questioning what consumerism is and actually gives us through its product design. I like to make the unique and one-off out of the mass-manufactured.

Do you always start the design process with recycled garments?
In the beginning it was very much about the "rejected branded product" that I'd seek to reinvent; holes and stains and a cracked faded print were the apple of my eye. Now it's evolved into dead stock and customizing archives for companies through the "DrNoki4" initiative to bring sustainable art/design into their agenda for corporate change. When I create for them, I'm still able to exhibit the creations as art. That is very important to me.

Do you have a research process?
My research process is simply about what is now! Not on trend, produced and consumed, and left for dead in landfill. At this point I can relax into my collage of customizing techniques.

Please describe your work art directing for Buddhist Punk.
Art directing for the Buddhist Punk label and creating the DrNoki4BP label has been a brilliant modern evolution for me. They basically choose pieces from their vast archive of 15 years and presented small batches of it to me, so I can then just get "Nokiing" it up into a new directional beast for them. Because it is their archive they are familiar with the design process used to create it, and they produce it sustainably utilizing what stock and warehouse build-up they have. With this initiative, I'm really able to focus on the NHS (Noki House of Sustain) idea of "Street Couture Culture" I set up for Lulu Kennedy's Fashion East in 2008.

What kind of brief/constraints/direction/market do you work to?
I'd say a new Wave Rave Generation looking to preserve intelligent stylish mankind.

What are your sources of inspiration?
Inspiration comes from looking and finding humor in the bizarre side of street life, because you will never find it in the High Street. So look up and down all other streets you find yourself walking upon.

How important is the research to the design process?
My research is my faith in what my art brings to me. It's one big rehabilitation to the kid I once was; billboarding the brand, watching the brand, judging brands worn, seeking the brand, so I could rave in the brand. Somewhere in the smoke, lasers, and sweat, Noki came to me as a way to sustain the original rave I am committed to.

How do you collate your research?
I've made hundreds of thousands of one-off pieces in my practice from once rejected designs. Was it bad design that rejected it? No, not necessarily, just a human need to consume through modern consumerist addiction. That's modern life.

Noki is my research into the human endeavor to be clothed.

Interview
Christopher Raeburn

Christopher Raeburn is a British fashion designer with a unique and innovative approach to creating menswear, womenswear, and accessories collections. A graduate of London's prestigious Royal College of Art, Christopher became known for his re-appropriation of military fabrics and in particular for iconic outerwear created from decommissioned parachutes. The "RE-MADE" ethos still guides and influences every aspect of the Christopher Raeburn design and development process; a Christopher Raeburn product is defined by distinctive aesthetic, meticulous detail, considered functionality, and sustainable intelligence.

Christopher's pioneering work has brought sustainable design to a mainstream fashion audience and presents a new definition of luxury with integrity. The brand currently has over 60 stockists worldwide and has received an amazing array of media coverage nationally and internationally, reflecting an unusually balanced combination of high concept and commercial awareness. Raeburn's AW10 collection propelled the brand to new heights: *US Vogue* featured the Inuit coat in a feature on sustainable fashion, informing all to "remember the four R's: reduce, reuse, recycle and Raeburn."

How do you start the research process?
I've always been interested in military history, and I still do a lot of research in this area. I have always and will always seek out materials and artifacts from military archives as a starting point for my design work. However I'm also very fascinated by environments, and most of my research starts by looking at specific places and cultures.

What kind of brief/constraints/direction/market do you work to?
It's important that I hold true to my values, which are most succinctly expressed in the RE-MADE aspect of what we do. Having said that, I also want to create an accessible wearable offering for our customers, so I try to find creative ways to integrate aspects of the RE-MADE concept through the collection or to reflect our commitment to RE-MADE through the use of other sustainable/recycled materials; most notably we use recycled polyester to create several of our best-selling and most accessible outerwear styles. It's not easy to hold true to this principle particularly as we grow, but I want to make sure that sustainability and integrity of purpose remain part of the DNA.

Do you set themes? If so, how and where do you work?
We have our seasonal concepts, but we also segment the range into three broad categories, RE-MADE, British, and Lightweight.

A small range of RE-MADE pieces lead the seasonal concept, focusing on the re-appropriation of a diverse range of military fabrics and garments.

British is derived from my interest in provenance and heritage and often features a number of signature outerwear styles, including bomber jackets, duffel coats, and parkas, made in British fabrics and/or by British manufacturers.

The Lightweight category evolved from my use of parachute fabric to create outerwear; these were some of the first products that attracted real attention and interest in the brand, and they continue to be a staple in our spring/summer collections. This category has grown and developed to include knitwear, T-shirts, sweatshirts, shorts, and joggers all made in Portugal.

What are your sources of inspiration?

The forthcoming Spring/Summer 2016 collection was inspired by an anthropologist called Tom Harrison who spent a lot of time in Borneo in the 1930s and was then sent back in during the Japanese occupation; he helped build a resistance movement among the local tribes to force out the Japanese; so the starting point is an aspect of military history, but then the landscapes, jungle, and wildlife of Borneo have also become a major influence on the collection.

Do you have sources that you repeat or revisit in seasons or collections?

Well, as I mentioned, there is always a military aspect to what I do, even if it is quite subtle.

How important is the research to the design process?

The collections quite literally wouldn't exist without it; it's the research that uncovers the materials that then get interpreted into the RE-MADE pieces that then guide the rest of the development process.

What advice would you give to anyone interested in a career in fashion/fashion forecasting?

Be very flexible, look for alternatives and new ideas in unexpected places, and try to maintain a healthy balance between creativity and commercial relevance.

Do you have a signature style?

It's more a detail than a style; we have a particular way of applying grosgrain to our lightweight hoodies and other garments

Menswear from Christopher Raeburn's Spring/Summer 2016 collection "Borneo."

Womenswear from Christopher Raeburn's Spring/Summer 2016 collection "Sarawak."

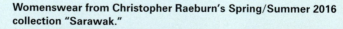

that was derived from the pattern of the original parachutes. I think it is very distinct.

Do you ever design a collection with one person in mind?

Well, I suppose we have people we feel represent what we do and who we like to see wearing our clothes, but I don't like to be too prescriptive. It's about finding a way to be cohesive and clear while ensuring that different parts of the collection can appeal to different individuals and cultures.

How do you collate your research?

I pull together a seasonal brief as a starting point, which I then share with the team, and they add to it and then we develop it together.

How important is the marketing and promotion of a collection to its success?

It's vital; people need to understand the narrative flow of the collection and feel drawn to the sense of style as well as the individual pieces we are creating. Film, photography, and words all need to support the actual garments, and we do our best to think holistically about this, so each season people can venture into a world, not just buy an item of clothing.

You've been interested in working with salvaged fabrics since being an undergraduate student. Where did this interest in upcycling come from? How important is it to you?

It was more coincidental than anything; as I say, I always had an interest in military history and I just think the military produce some incredibly innovative and amazing fabrics for all sorts of purposes; more to the point they also massively overproduce. I've always said that it just made sense to take something of which there is an excess and re-imagine it in a new context; thankfully it seems to make sense to other people as well.

Menswear from Christopher Raeburn's Spring/Summer 2016 collection "Borneo."

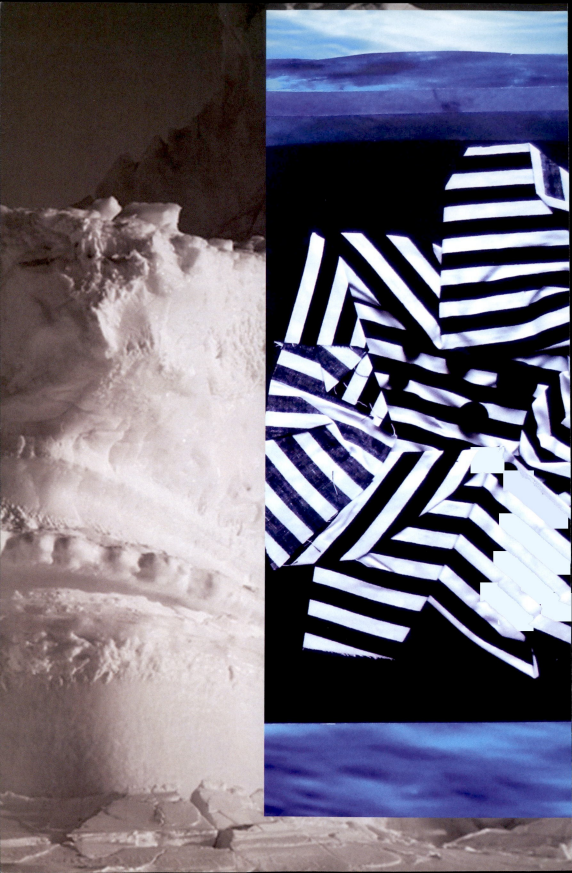

Compiling
your research

3

So far, you have discovered what research is and why you need it as a designer. You have also learned where you can find it and the many sources of inspiration that are available to you. In this chapter, we explain how to piece together the information you have found. We explain the format of a sketchbook and examine different approaches to compiling your research, from drawing and collage to deconstruction and analysis. The chapter uses different examples of sketchbook work to illustrate the many styles you can adopt. It also discusses how to move the research forward and begin to focus on key elements on moodboards and concept boards, in preparation for the design process.

"As a fashion designer I was aware that I was not an artist because I was creating something that was made to be sold, marketed, used and ultimately discarded." Tom Ford

Examples of moodboards and storyboards (see also pages 70–73).

The sketchbook

As a designer, you need to explore and experiment with the idea of a sketchbook and how you compile your research. A sketchbook is generally the place where you can collate and process all the information you have collected, and it can become a very personal and individual space for ideas.

Assembling your research

Sketchbooks have traditionally been collated in book format with designers choosing the format and size that they take. A sketchbook can, however, also be gradually gathered and created into something that is later bound, allowing the designer the opportunity to select and edit material as necessary.

Research can also be presented as a series of storyboards. This approach often is used in a design studio, where images, photographs, drawings, fabrics, and trimmings are stuck to an inspiration wall or a series of moodboards.

The sketchbook can also be a tool to illustrate a collection and describe to others the journey you have taken. This information is often essential, as it shows how you perceive the world around you and demonstrates your ability to be a creative thinker. You also can share it with others in a design studio to ensure that you are all working to a common set of themes.

Research books are not merely scrapbooks filled with tear sheets and photographs, but they are a place of learning, recording, and processing information. A sketchbook should explore and experiment with a variety of ways in which the information can be presented.

Sketchbooks

You can purchase sketchbooks in a wide variety of sizes, paper weights, colors, and bindings. You can also make them for yourself, allowing you to work on different qualities of paper and then edit and order the work before binding it. Additionally, you can create a sketchbook in a second-hand format, by working in an old novel or textbook, perhaps using the text as a background to the theme of the research.

DEVELOPMENT. .... ERING. LOOK 1

DEVELOPING A SILHOUETTE.

Drawing

Drawing is a fundamental process and skill that you must explore and perfect. It is an ideal way to record information on the spot; in other words, it is a good way to gather primary research. By using a variety of different drawing media—for example, pencils, inks, and paints—you are able to exploit the qualities and styles of line, texture, tone, and color that can be gained from your sources of inspiration and add depth to your research and design. To draw the whole or part of an object or picture you have sourced helps you understand the shapes and forms that are contained within it. This, in turn, enables you to translate these lines into a design or to see them clearly when you are cutting a pattern. Brush marks and textures explored through drawing may also translate into fabric references in your designs. Throughout the creative research process, you will continue to understand and develop your visual language skills, and drawing is just one part of that.

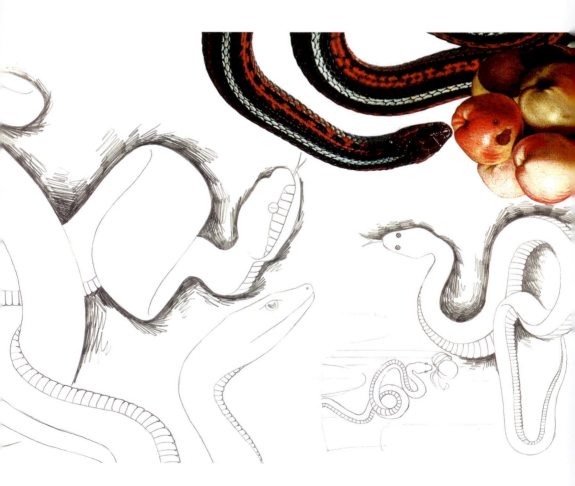

Techniques for drawing

Familiarity with varied drawing materials will provide you with a stronger ability to interpret and exploit your research and the analysis of your inspiration.

Capturing and recording ideas using varied materials and techniques is an important part of the sketchbook process, and the use of broad and varied media will help to direct and advance the research process.

Using creative drawing techniques and exploring research and analysis with mixed media combinations can help you convey a style and create an aesthetic within your own creative work. Additionally, it enables you to develop your own visual language.

There are many different drawing materials and ways in which to apply them, and it is only through trial and error that you will discover the ones that work best for you. Listed here are some of the materials that you can use when capturing and recording ideas and developing your drawings.

Drawing utensils

Graphite pencils

When you think of drawing, the first thing that comes to mind is the use of a pencil; its varied grades from hard to soft allow you to easily create monochrome tonal and linear representations of the subject matter as well as interpret these drawings into early design ideas. You can use graphite pencils to create a variety of textures within a drawing; techniques to explore include smudging and highlighting with an eraser or using cross-hatching techniques to add texture and indicate fabric or pattern. H pencils are hard and B pencils are soft. The higher the number, the harder or softer the pencil. The pencil in the middle of the hard/soft spectrum is HB. (In the US, pencils are graded as follows: #1 = B; #2 = HB; #2½ = F; #3 = H; #4 = 2H.)

Example of a design drawing using graphite pencils.

Drawing utensils

Ballpoint and fine-liner pens

Sketching with a ballpoint or fine-liner pen can produce a similar result to a hard graphite pencil, but often requires you to work in a more linear and graphic style. You can sketch using techniques such as continuous line, straight line only, or single line representation of objects. The use of a pen can offer varied styles and approaches to drawing and can often enhance the clarity of a design sketch.

Colored pencils

Colored pencils provide you with a quick and clean method of sketching and introducing color. Working with colored pencils allows you to add in much more detail and texture to a drawing; and if you work with watercolor pencils, the addition of a brush and water allows you to blend and highlight effects. The water dissolves the color and introduces light and a transparent effect to the drawing. The water also allows for blending and mixing of color on the page and can create depth and tone to any observational or design drawing.

Pastels and Conté pencils

Pastels are created using dry, ground pigment mixed with a binder to form a paste, which, when hardened, forms crayons or sticks. Pastels allow you to create soft chalk-like marks and a velvety finish. Using your fingers often helps when applying color with pastels, and color can be gradually built up with strong highlights and smoky tones. A Conté pencil, which is made up of chalk that is bound with gum and oil, allows you to create a more intense and thick line. This is a harder, more precise medium than a pastel but can be used successfully alongside pastels to create (large) expressive drawings and illustrations. However, these pencils can be messy and indelicate for finer drawings and illustrations and need to be used in conjunction with a fixative spray to prevent smudging.

Inks, nibs, and brushes

Ink is a liquid medium and has an intense pigment capacity. When used, it can create wonderful intense color with fluid lines; when mixed with water, it can offer a more soft and transparent look. Used with brushes, it can cover much more of a drawing and give color and tone to a large space. When you use a nib (or tip), it can be treated the same as a pen, giving sharper and more precise marks. Inks are a great medium to explore, because used with wet and dry paper, they also react differently; used in combination with pencils and Conté crayons or even bleach, inks can give real depth and contrast to the designer's sketchbook.

Watercolor paints

Watercolor paints are based on the techniques of using water to create transparency and soft fluid renderings in your drawings. Using watercolor paints allows you to apply color in layers, building up tones and shades gradually to show texture, light, and form. Using washes and allowing them to dry before applying further color or dry media such as pencils or pastels is a great way to experiment with texture and fabric rendering.

Marker pens and brush-tip pens

Working with marker or brush-tip pens is the most modern way of hand-rendering a drawing. They are used for the design process particularly because they are quick, clean, and graphic in their finish. Marker pens come in all different colors and shades, and a good design student should always have at least two flesh-tone markers in slightly different shades for design drawing.

Collage

The use of collage in your research is another approach to collating information from different sources—for example, photographs, magazine clippings, and printouts from the Internet.

The images you select need not necessarily have anything immediately in common. A good collage will explore a variety of elements that have their own strengths and qualities, but in combination present new directions as a whole. When you are working with images, do not be restricted by the shape you have, for example, a rectangle or square; cut out the shapes and collage

them together in a creative way instead. Think of Monty Python's collaged titles and the work of pop artist Peter Blake, who created the album cover for The Beatles' *Sgt. Pepper's Lonely Hearts Club Band*, when putting the information together. Scale, placement, and selection are skills that you will start to learn as you explore this technique in your sketchbook.

Collage

Collage is the artistic composition of sticking bits of paper and photographs to a surface, but the word originally derives from the French word for *gluing*.

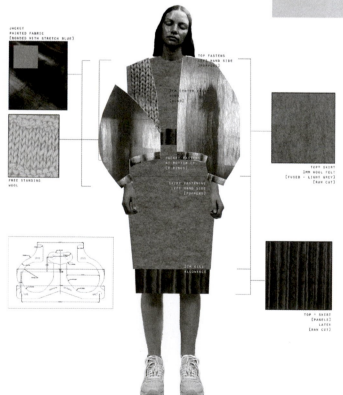

Images from student sketchbooks exploring the use of the collage technique.

LOOK THREE

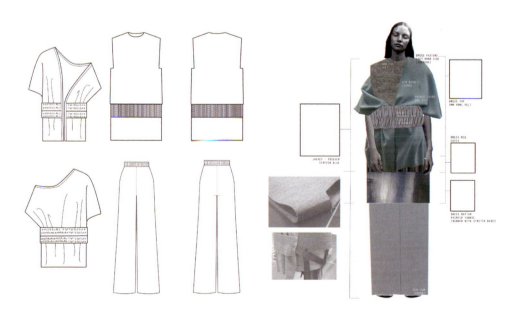

LOOK FOUR

Juxtaposition and deconstruction

Juxtapose means to place or deal with things close together for comparison or a contrasting effect. In terms of your research and design, this might relate to placing images and fabrics side by side on your moodboard or in your sketchbook.

Juxtaposition

Whereas collage is about cutting and sticking images together to create new ideas, juxtaposition describes the process whereby you place images and fabrics side by side on the page.

Juxtaposition is a method that can often bring together disparate elements that share similarities—for example, the spiral shape of an ammonite fossil and a spiral staircase. Or the images may be suggestive of a fabric quality—for example, the textures of a starfish and coral may bring to mind an embossed or embellished fabric. You may bring two seemingly unrelated images together because they are aesthetically pleasing together and may suggest new possibilities in the research or design process.

Deconstruction

To deconstruct or disassemble your research is to consider looking at the information from a new viewpoint or perspective. It may simply mean using a viewfinder and drawing an aspect of the object so that you focus on a detail, arriving at an abstract idea from the original source. But it may also mean breaking up the information like a jigsaw puzzle and reassembling it differently to create new lines, shapes, and abstract forms to work from.

Disassemblage is also a process that relates to working with actual garments as a source of inspiration. In this technique you can take existing clothes apart and analyze how they have been created, perhaps taking patterns from them and looking at the construction details, which could then be translated into your own design ideas. This method of research was previously discussed in more detail on pages 60–61.

Viewfinder

A viewfinder is a creative tool that allows you to conceal an object and then expose or view only a part of it. It can be made from a simple piece of card or paper; all you need to do is cut a small square window into the center of it. The window can be as small or as large as you wish, but the point is to offer you a view of only part of the object or image that you have sourced.

This Maison Martin Margiela artisanal jacket from Autumn/Winter
2011–12 has been deconstructed to reveal the internal construction.

Cross-referencing

Your research may be initially quite abstract and varied, with many seemingly unrelated references sourced and explored. Methods like drawing, collage, and juxtaposition are great for collating and experimenting with information, but cross-referencing your research is a technique that gets you to look for related visual references or ones that complement each other. These references can then be grouped into early themes or concepts for you to explore further in the design process.

One example shown here demonstrates how a Naum Gabo sculpture and an Issey Miyake garment have similar qualities, for instance. All of these references come from different sources, but by bringing them together, you can see how they relate to one another and form new directions for you to design from.

It is this mix of sources with similar qualities that is the essence of cross-referencing—and an essential part of any good research and the early analysis of it.

Images demonstrating the similarities between a Naum Gabo sculpture and an Issey Miyake garment.

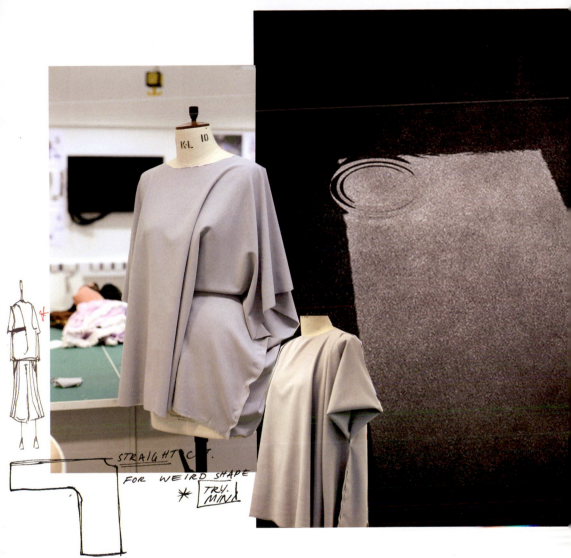

STRAIGHT CUT.
FOR WEIRD SHAPE
✱ TRY.
MIND

Student sketchbook demonstrating cross-referenced sources.

Analysis of research

As you begin to explore your research and compile ideas through collage and cross-referencing, you will start to see potential directions for your design. You will already have gathered information regarding shapes, textures, details, color, print, and perhaps historical references as part of your research. Now it's important that you begin to use your research and analyze it in terms of early design sketches.

Why is analysis useful?

Early analysis requires you to draw shapes from the sources you have explored and to experiment with mixed-media sketches, close-up and silhouette studies, linear drawings, and details for construction.

These sketches should also explore ideas for texture, pattern, and possible embellishments. The drawings need not necessarily be done on a figure and can simply be interpretations of the information that you have collected.

Color should be something that you consider and explore through the use of mixed media, using the research as inspiration and extracting possible ideas for color palettes and combinations. The research should contain some early ideas of texture and possible fabric manipulation, and therefore, these should form part of the early analysis for fabric design. You must begin to source and edit samples and trims that perhaps have similar qualities to the inspiration and show how your research has informed your thought processes into textural fabric ideas.

Another key stage of analysis is to try to translate early shapes from your research into quarter-scale pattern experiments or modeling on a stand (see pages 104–105). This is a three-dimensional approach to analysis, and by experimenting with and translating the information gathered, you will begin to see the potential for garment ideas and record this through photography and sketching. This extremely valuable part of the research and design process is explored more fully in chapter 4.

Student sketchbook exploring early 2D and 3D design ideas from historical research.

Focus on key elements

Through the early stages of research, compilation, and analysis, you will start to have a much clearer direction and focus for your design concept. Each of these stages will give you important inspiration and information to work with as a designer. The analysis will draw out some of the key elements that you must consider when designing a collection, such as shape, color, fabric, details, print, and embellishment.

This next stage is simply about focusing your mind using your sketchbook and creating a series of pages that clearly identify the elements that you wish to work from.

This focus also allows other people to interact with your vision; in other words, if you were working as a team, this is the point at which other members of the team could respond to the direction that the research was taking and add their input or suggestions for the collection.

This focusing of the key elements can also be presented as a series of mood-, story-, or concept boards.

SHAVING OF THE HAIR EXPLORAT

BRA PANNELLING

DESIGN DEVELOPMENT

Student sketchbook illustrating key influences and their use for design ideas.

Exercise 5
Focus research pages

In this exercise, you need to highlight some of the key aspects of your research and compile a set of concept or focus pages.

First, remember what you have explored and researched from the various sources of inspiration (see Exercise 2). Then try to select and edit the best elements that could be developed further or that relate to early design opportunities.

Now try to compile something that relates to each of the categories discussed previously (and listed again, below) so that your research and design start from a broad set of ideas and topics:

- shapes and structures
- details
- color
- textures
- print and embellishment
- historical influences
- cultural influences
- contemporary trends

The point of gathering, grouping, and focusing the research into a set of pages or storyboards is so that you can review the inspiration—often with others—before moving forward in the design process.

It is a good idea to make copies of the research gathered during Exercise 2, as this will allow you to cut and paste the best elements together into new juxtaposing or cross-referenced spreads without losing the original images.

Make sure that you have images and fabric swatches that tell the story of the research so far. Color, texture, shape, and details are all important foundations for good design, and this exercise is designed to get you to consider the elements that you have found and perhaps also to review what might still be missing or require further investigation.

The focus pages you create can point to different directions and possible combinations that might arise from your research, and don't necessarily need to be similar depending on how broad and diverse your research has been. But the focus pages will at least help to understand the key elements that you will need to move the research and design process forward.

Remember: While these pages are designed to form a rough and experimental part of the sketchbook, they can lead into more refined moodboards or storyboards, as you will see on the following pages.

Moodboards

Mood-, story-, and concept boards are a way of presenting focused design information to others, whether they are your clients, financial backers, a team of designers, or your tutors. These boards can be described as the front cover to your collection and should tell the story of your research by presenting a few selected pieces of information. Their name even suggests what they are trying to do—that is, to create a mood, tell a story, and explore a concept. They are an edited, refined, and considered distillation of your research.

Making a board of your own

Mood-, story-, and concept boards are generally presented on board, pinboard, or mount card, as this is a durable format. However, if your moodboards are to be included in a portfolio, it would be better to use a thick paper because it is less bulky. The size depends on the use, as these boards are often large scale when used in a design studio but could be smaller for academic purposes.

All that you need is a simple layout and composition of images and fabric, and you can even use the techniques explored in research collation as a way of presenting ideas. For example, consider the use of collage and juxtaposition (described earlier in this chapter).

Market

At the start of your research, you should have considered who you are designing for as a result of the brief you are answering. In terms of the moodboard, it is important to suggest the client in the images—in other words, to present images that might reflect the client's perceived lifestyle or to simply use the brand's logo.

More examples of moodboards and storyboards(see also pages 88–89).

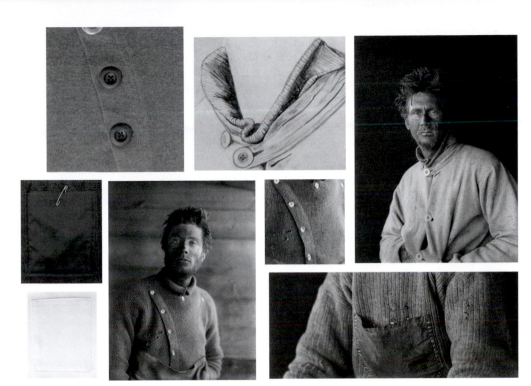

Key elements

The key elements that a moodboard should contain are as follows.

Color palette
Colors need to be clearly identified through the use of swatches of color. These can be paint shade cards, Pantone shade cards, or cards that you mix. It is important to present an image that complements and supports the colors that you have selected.

Reference to theme/research
The purpose of including a reference to theme/research is to show the viewer where you have come from in the journey of your research. It needs to focus on your edit of the most important images and references used for your inspiration; for example, if you have explored styles from the 1920s, then you should include images that suggest this.

Fabric
During the research process, you should have begun to collect fabric swatches and ideas for print, embellishment, trims, and so on. The moodboard needs to include suggested samples to support the developing ideas.

Key words and text
It often helps to have descriptive words or short paragraphs of text that help to describe the theme or story of the collection.

Styling imagery

Styling imagery is closely linked to the market, as it helps to present your designs within a lifestyle context. Selected images can bring an ideal character to the collection. But styling imagery also presents a whole package. The environment or landscape that the photograph has been taken in; the colors, props, and styling; hair and make-up—all may well contribute to creating an ideal image for your collection.

COLOUR AND FABRICS
EXPLORATION AND RESEARCH

Final Coulour Way

Sketchbook layout

There are no hard-and-fast rules on how to lay out your research in your sketchbook. You do not need to cover every part of the page with your research and drawings; often the negative space adds to the dynamism of a page and how it is read. Different edges and irregular sizes can all add to the composition and layout of the information. Allow the different sources to interact through collage, but also have space in the juxtaposition layout.

Balance

Often a wonderful drawing and a single photograph are all that is needed across a double page to explain an idea and present something visually stimulating. The sketchbook should be about balance and so can have both quiet and busy moments in terms of information and sources of inspiration.

Ultimately, the sketchbook is about inspiration and exploration, so it should never be so preciously laid out as to restrict these essential practices. Here are some examples of different sketchbook pages that explore further the ideas discussed in this chapter.

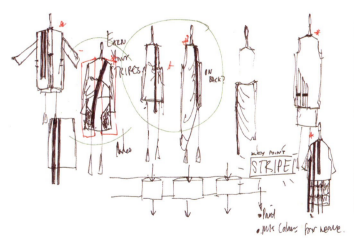

Student sketchbooks showing various forms of layout and composition, as well as early exploratory design analysis, sketching, and use of collage (see also pages 92–93).

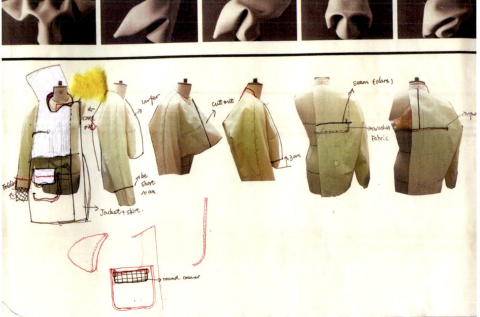

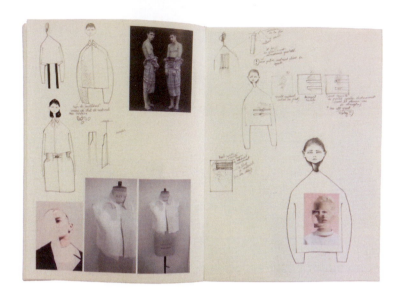

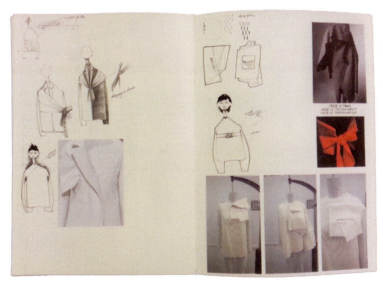

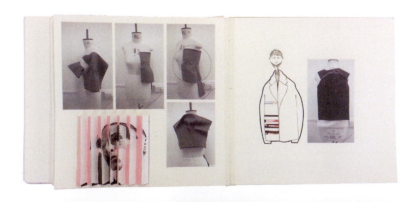

boxer's equipment training ground.

Handwraps
Another kind of
hand protecting
equipment in
boxing.

injury of a boxer

Cigarette card from Portobello
Market

Beautiful detailed boxer glove on
Portobello Market.

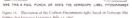

WAS THIS A FOUL PUNCH, OR DOES THE VERISCOPE LIBEL FITZSIMMONS?

Figure 18. Illustration of the Corbett-Fitzsimmons fight, based on Veriscope film
frames, San Francisco Examiner, July 13, 1897.

Figure 9. Eadweard Muybridge, Nude Male Athlete Boxing, plate 336, Animal
Locomotion (1887). (Library of Congress, Prints and Photographs Division.)

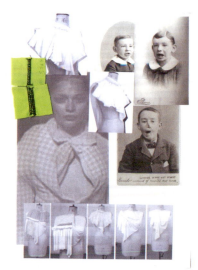

Interview

Marchesa

British born Georgina Chapman and Keren Craig have built a fashion empire defined by elegant eveningwear and one-of-a-kind couture designs. The duo met at Chelsea College of Art and Design in London. Georgina's draping and design expertise paired with Keren's textile creations resulted in a business partnership and the establishment of Marchesa in 2004. With the extravagant and eccentric fashion icon and Italian heiress as their muse, Georgina and Keren's beautifully crafted runway collections and accessories line fuse exquisite detailing with supreme femininity. Coveted not only by celebrities, but by women of all ages, Marchesa continues to be the centerpiece of iconic red carpet moments and high-end fashion alike. Based in New York, the Marchesa collections are presently available worldwide.

How do you start the research process?
We create large moodboard collages at the beginning of each season to organize all of our inspirations for the collection. From there, we begin to ideate the different looks and how we will interpret the inspirations.

What kind of brief/constraints/direction/ market do you work to?
We do not design with particular trends or constraints in mind, instead focusing on our core customer and creating beautiful looks that will inspire her.

Do you set themes? If so, how and where do you work?
Once we come up with a general concept for the collection, we gather imagery, build large moodboards, create color stories, drape silhouettes, and find beading inspiration that connects to our references. Intricate embroideries are a Marchesa signature, and each season in our atelier, we create custom embroideries that tie back to that season's inspiration. We are always exploring new techniques and one-off textural embroideries to bring unique detailing to every collection.

What are your sources of inspiration?
Inspiration comes together through various influences, imagery, textures, fabrics, and references. It is often drawn from a piece of art, a book, and travel.

Do you have sources that you repeat or revisit in seasons or collections?
The brand evolves each season according to our inspiration for that collection, but we always stay true to our aesthetic and with that do look at previous seasons for inspiration. Travel in particular is a constant source of inspiration; the location may change, but the romance and adventure of travel [are] always central to our designs.

How would you describe your signature style?
Marchesa is glamorous and feminine, and our goal is always to make women feel their most beautiful. We do not focus on trends when designing for Marchesa; instead, we look for new ways to bring our signature romantic and feminine vision to life each season.

Do you ever design a collection with one person in mind?
We always have the Marchesa woman in mind while designing the collection: she is confident, elegant, and embodies a true sense of identity.

What are the different considerations you make when designing your main line, Marchesa and Marchesa Notte?
We were very lucky to be able to launch Marchesa and its sister collection, Marchesa Notte, at the same time. The lines are truly a complement to each other, offering our customers looks for day, night, and a range of occasions. Each line is designed with the same Marchesa woman in mind, highlighting impeccable craftsmanship and unique design details.

What advice would you give to anyone interested in a career in fashion design?
We are very lucky to be doing what we love; not everyone can say that. We think the most important thing for anyone interested in any career is to do something that you feel truly passionate about. With passion comes creativity, drive, and focus, which are the grounds for a successful career.

Marchesa haute couture Autumn/Winter 2015–16.

Marchesa Spring/Summer 2016.

Interview

Nigel Luck

Having been trained in design at the RCA, Nigel has balanced his career between working as a design consultant in London, Paris, and Italy and lecturing in design at prestigious courses in the UK, which include Central St. Martins College of Art and Design, University of Westminster (Course Director), and now London College of Fashion (MA Fashion Design Technology, Womenswear).

As a fashion educator, what is your approach to research within the design process, and what importance do you give it?
As a rule, I feel the research is the initial starting point to encourage creativity, knowledge, and the whole design process. It is of extreme importance.

What does research mean to you? How do you encourage students to present their research?
Students are undergoing a learning process and their research, whether supervised or personal, is a vital ingredient to inform them and widen their knowledge. The students can present this in any form they want, but it should be personalized. Often certain presentations seem more modern than others; currently, the moodboard is considered cliché, but is still popular in industry. The important issue is to put together visuals and words that say something and have a personal take. Arguably, a gorilla could find an impressive image or photograph, but the student should be contextualizing this image in relation to other images to express their viewpoint.

You have worked on several prestigious fashion courses in the UK. What are the differences in the approaches to research and design between under- and postgraduate studies?
One would like to think that postgraduate students understand this better and produce better results, but this may not always be the case. Postgraduate students can be from all over the world, so research may be an area that has been overlooked by their tutors. Some of these students are returning from industry, and this experience may have encouraged them to take shortcuts and to get them into bad habits which undermine the researching process.

What changes have you seen in the education of fashion over the years?
There are too many fashion students being trained, but at least they are being encouraged to specialize in other areas than design. Education is delivering the best it can with limited resources. The downside may be that the large costs are prohibitive to students progressing from BA to MA.

What is the (design) philosophy of the MA Fashion Design Technology Womenswear at London College of Fashion?
To nurture creativity from two dimensions to three dimensions, and to the highest standards.

When you look at student application portfolios, what do you look for?
IDEAS!!!! Then I worry about the details, such as age, skillset, etc.

What in your opinion makes a successful fashion student?
Talent, but more importantly, personal style, image, and charisma.

What does a newly graduated designer need to consider on entering the workplace?
They need to know that they have not necessarily been employed to turn the company upside down. They are a contributor and are with others that have worked there a lot longer.

What advice would you give to anyone interested in a career in fashion? And what advice would you give to a fashion graduate (under- or postgraduate)?
It's a fabulous profession, but you will need to be determined and to survive a few disappointments.

Three outfits from the graduate MA Fashion Design Technology Womenswear course at London College of Fashion shown during London Fashion Week Autumn/Winter 2015–16.

Designing from your research

Designing is about mixing up known elements in new and exciting ways to create fresh and original products. It is also about exploiting the full potential from the in-depth research gathered and translating this information successfully. In this chapter, we explain the fundamental stages of translating research into design. Understanding what the design development processes are and how they affect the creative outcomes is essential to being a successful fashion designer.

We explore how to translate early ideas from your research into shapes and structures on the body, using model-and-drape techniques. As we move into the area of garment development and design, it is essential that you have a basic understanding of fabric and its different qualities. This chapter further explores the silhouette and function of a garment and looks at the use of color and print. It also provides you with several exercises to help you generate design ideas and evolve a collection. The final stages of the design process are to refine and edit your ideas to create a cohesive and complete collection.

> "Fashion is a form of ugliness so intolerable that we have to alter it every six months."
> Oscar Wilde

An embellishment by Martin Margiela Spring/Summer 2016 using unconventional components.

Bridging the gap

So far, all the work you have explored has been focused on the research and inspiration for the design process, gathering ideas and experimenting with information in your sketchbooks. But what about the design? How do you start to design and to bridge the gap between the inspiration and the actual design process?

Certainly, working on the stand using recycled garments and the model-and-drape technique (see pages 104–105) will provide you with some key ideas for shape and silhouette that you can use in the early translation of research into design. But you should also consider two other approaches to help you bridge the gap and start the design process. These are by collaging your research onto figures (page 103) and using photomontage with drapery (see pages 106–107).

Layout paper

Layout paper is slightly transparent paper that you can use with templates to draw design development ideas quickly. Using it, you can trace off the figure easily each time and overlay other ideas. It does not work well with wet media, however, as it tends to buckle.

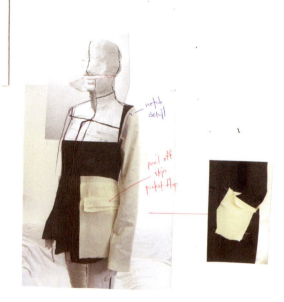

Student research sketchbooks showing collage on figure.

Exercise 6

Collaging your research onto figures

Collaging your research onto figures is a quick and quite literal way to translate your research into design ideas. This approach is not really used in industry very often, but it is an ideal technique to try as a novice designer.

It requires you to make several copies of different pages of your research, so use a photocopier or scanner to help you at this stage. You then need to draw out a series of fashion figures or templates (discussed in chapter 5) onto layout paper or directly into your sketchbook. You can then begin to simply cut and collage different aspects of your photocopied research directly onto the figures. This technique allows you to immediately see the design potential of some of the images. Perhaps spiral shells translate into the shape of a skirt or floral leaves into a dress, for instance.

The technique does require you to consider several anchor points on the body, which you need to start developing your collages from. These are

- neck
- shoulders
- bust
- waist
- hips

You also should consider arms and legs (that is, sleeves and trousers) as points to develop from.

This technique concentrates essentially on the possibilities of shapes and silhouettes on the body but may also suggest color, print, and texture, depending on the research images used in this process.

Model and drape

Modeling and draping are processes of creating garment patterns and garment shapes through manipulating fabric on a stand or mannequin. By folding, pleating, gathering, and draping a fabric onto a three-dimensional stand, a designer can work on more complex shapes and techniques that are often too difficult to develop in the more conventional manner of flat pattern cutting or by drawing alone. Draping fabric does not require the aid of a garment pattern to create designs, but you can choose to incorporate part of an existing pattern in the preparation.

Draping on the stand

Draping fabric at this stage of the design process is a good way to start the early translation of ideas gathered through your research. Taking abstract shapes from what has inspired you and exploring the potential on a mannequin provide a much more expressive way of developing ideas for garments than drawing alone; this process can be described as akin to sculpting fabric onto the body.

Draping on the stand is also a technique that can help you begin to understand the relationships between a research sketch and a three-dimensional form. It is often difficult to see how a two-dimensional drawing will translate onto the body, so by modeling on a stand, you can begin to explore the idea more clearly.

When you use this technique, it is important to still be aware of the body and how the fabric relates to it. Volume and shape are important, but does the shape flatter the natural contours of the body?

Recording the work on the stand is equally important. Drawing and photographing the ideas as they grow and change are integral parts of the early stages of research and design development and should form an important part of the design aspect of the sketchbook.

By its very definition, draping is about fabric, folds, and movement, so it is essential that you have a basic understanding of a fabric's qualities and characteristics. The quality, weight, structure, and handle of the fabric all play an important part in how something looks and reacts on the stand in the model-and-drape process, as we explore later in this chapter.

Volume

In fashion terms, volume relates to excess fabric in a garment; a garment said to have volume often moves away from the natural curves of the body, creating new silhouettes.

"It's more like engineering than anything else. It's finding the limits of what you can do when wrapping the body in fabric. Everything evolves. Nothing is strictly defined."
John Galliano
(Galliano, Colin McDowell)

Student sketchbook work exploring model-and-drape techniques and development.

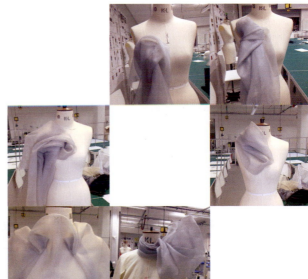

Photomontage with drapery

The technique of using photomontage with drapery expands on the three-dimensional experiments that you began to explore on the stand. You can now use the photographs and drawings of these experiments on a two-dimensional figure in your sketchbook.

You need to use fashion figure templates again and either layout paper or pages in your sketchbook. This time, instead of using images from your research to collage onto figures, you can use the photographs and drawings that you made of drapery on the stand. Try to move the images around the figure and change the scale and placement. Repeating images on the same figure can also be a successful way of gaining further design ideas from your initial experiments on the stand.

Drawing on the photomontage figures can add greater depth and may open up other avenues as to the eventual design outcome. You still need to consider the same anchor points on the body for this technique, however.

You can then further work both techniques of collaging the research directly and working with photographs of draped stand-work into early design ideas by redrawing and refining the garments using layout paper or sketchbook pages.

You should now be well underway with your first design ideas and successfully bridging the gap between the research process and the design process.

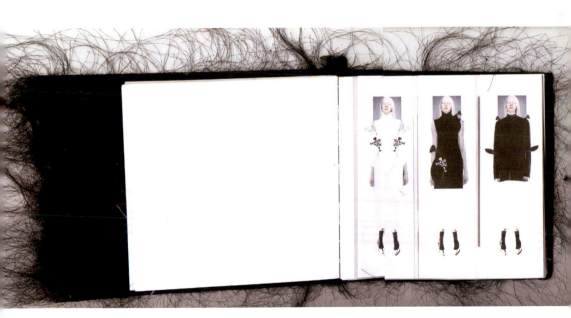

Student sketchbook exploring modeled stand-work and photographic montage techniques.

Design development elements

As already discussed, research is guided through a set of required elements or components that you must consider and gather information for: components such as shape and structure, texture and color, and historical influences.

These elements now become essential in developing your ideas into garment shapes and details, determining fabric qualities, using color and print, and following the creative direction that the collection is ultimately going to take.

There is perhaps also an order in which you should begin to consider these elements as part of the design process. By exploring all of them, you will achieve a greater and more in-depth understanding of your collection and the concept that you have developed.

Design elements

- Silhouette
- Proportion and line
- Function
- Details
- Color
- Fabric
- Print and embellishment
- Historic references
- Contemporary trends
- Market, levels, and genres in fashion

Silhouette

The silhouette of a garment is often the first thing that the viewer will see and respond to when the garment is presented on the catwalk. Silhouette simply means the outline or shape that is cast around the body by a garment. It is essential to the development of a collection and needs to be seen from a distance before the details, fabric, or texture can be discerned. Closely allied with silhouette is volume. The fullness, bulk, or lack of it is readily seen in a garment style and its silhouette. A garment can also contain qualities of lightness or weight through the use of padded, heavy, or sheer fabrics, which will again affect the silhouette achieved.

When designing the silhouette, try to consider the garment from all angles (360 degrees) because the silhouette may not be obvious from the first front-view impression. Allegedly, Alexander McQueen always preferred to draw and design his clothes from the side rather than the front or the back.

Developing and refining a silhouette is important to the whole process of design, as it will unify and help create an identity for your collection. Inspiration for the silhouette should come from the different elements of your research, specifically from shapes and structures or perhaps from historical dress. Looking at abstract shapes in your research and then applying them to a figure are the first stages of basic design development.

Alexander Wang for Balenciaga Autumn/Winter 2015.

Viktor & Rolf haute couture Autumn/Winter 2015–16. Always unconventional, Viktor & Rolf dressed their models with pictures from the wall.

Historical silhouettes

Many notable and often dramatic silhouettes in historical dress provide insight into the changes regarding what was seen as the desirable body shape at a particular time. During the eighteenth century, the fashion was to accentuate the hourglass form of the body to the extreme through the use of corsets, enormous powdered wigs, and huge crinolines. Women's French court dress and the earliest known dressmaker, Rose Bertin, along with her patron, Marie Antoinette, epitomized this fashion. During the late nineteenth century, the Victorians picked up on this silhouette once again, using corsets and huge padded crinolines to increase the scale of the skirt and accentuate the tiny waist.

Christian Dior shocked the world after the Second World War with his New Look in 1947. His collection reintroduced the nipped-in waist and gathered full skirt of the Belle Époque (1871–1914), using much more luxurious fabrics. It was a move away from the more austere fashions of the war period and the rationing it brought. The second half of the twentieth century brought hem lines up, and exposing legs became much more acceptable. Designer Mary Quant created the mini skirt in the 1960s, and as they had in the 1920s, women subverted the fashion for the hourglass silhouette by flattening their busts and curves, and they began to wear their hair short.

More recently, designers such as Viktor & Rolf, Comme des Garçons, Gareth Pugh, and Rick Owens have played with the use of scale and proportion in their silhouettes, often moving away from the traditional aesthetics of the body's shape. Their work can be linked more closely with sculptural, even architectural, forms.

Proportion and line

The proportion of a garment refers to how the body is divided up, either through lines—horizontal, vertical, diagonal, curved, or straight—or through the use of blocks of color or texture and fabric. The combination of these elements can create infinite and diverse possibilities. The proportions of the body can be seen through the changes in waist, hem, and necklines, and are often judged by clients based on their own personal view of their bodies and what suits their body shape.

Proportion can also refer to the contrast of scale within a garment; the volume of the top half of a sleeve, for instance, might make the bottom half look smaller or tighter by comparison. The line of a garment generally relates to its cut and the placement of seams and darts. These can create visually interesting effects, such as lengthening the body or giving the illusion of a narrower waist. The empire line from the late-eighteenth century raised the waistline under the bust and gave the illusion of a lengthened body.

Bias cut dress by Richard Sorger Spring/Summer 2009.

Rules of proportion/line

1. Vertical lines tend to lengthen the body.
2. Horizontal lines widen the body.
3. Curved lines or lines cut on the bias create a more curvaceous and feminine look.
4. Straight lines tend to be seen as more masculine and structured.
5. Seams and darts are not standard and can be moved around the body.

Bias cut

A bias cut is created when you cut or drape a fabric on a 45-degree angle to the selvedge, or the horizontal or vertical woven threads called "the straight grain."

Function

The function of a garment refers to what it is: a dress, a skirt, trousers, or perhaps a jacket. The brief you are working toward will often give you guidelines as to what is expected at the end of the design process, so it is important that you are clear on what types of garments you are designing. Function can also relate to garments that have a purpose and specific demands; for example, when creating garments for the sportswear industry, you need to consider performance, fabric qualities, and the type of sport they are to be worn for. It is important at the design stage to know what types of garments you are designing and what purpose they need to serve.

A classic trench coat by Burberry, showing an example of functional clothing. The brand still retains function in its recent collections.

Details

A garment can have a wonderful silhouette and good line, but the details define and differentiate it from other designers' work. The details are what often clinch a sale. As clients inspect a garment more closely, they are able to see more than just the shape and cut, such as interesting fastenings, topstitching, unusual pockets, collar styles, and belts. These are all elements to be considered in the design process and allow you to explore more subtle changes and developments in similar garments in your collection.

Clever detailing is often seen and used more widely in menswear, as extreme silhouettes and bold fabrics are less likely to be used to create new and inventive designs for a largely conservative clientele.

A simple exercise you can do to explore this idea of detailing is to start by drawing six of the same basic shirt shapes. Then explore the possibilities of different detailing and design on each of the six different shirts (see the exercise on page 132 to develop your drawings further).

Types of detailing

- Topstitching and different methods of stitching
- Fastenings: zippers, buttons, hook-and-eye, eyelets, lace-up, straps, Velcro, press studs
- Collar, lapel, and cuff styles
- Yoke shapes
- Sleeve shapes
- Dress straps and necklines
- Pocket styles
- Belts
- Finishing of seams: bound, French, channel, raw

Color

Color is a fundamental consideration in the design process. It is often the first element that is noticed about a design and influences how that garment or collection is perceived. Color can often be the starting point of both the design process and of a collection. Choosing colors, or a palette for a collection, is one of the earliest decisions that you must make, as it will often dictate the mood or season you are working toward. It is therefore vital that you have a basic understanding of color theory and of how color can be created and coordinated. Although it is important to understand color, most designers do not choose their color palettes or schemes based on theories. Once you fully understand basic color theory and how to mix color (see Exercise 7), it is important to reflect on the original sources of inspiration for the direction you take your color palette. It may well be that you explore a variety of ideas using different color combinations before focusing on one group to design with.

Two images from Christian Dior haute couture Spring/Summer 2015 utilizing vivid color.

Exercise 7
Working with the color wheel

Creating a color wheel is an exercise you can try yourself; it will help you understand the basics of mixing color. You need to have tubes of either watercolor or gouache paint, water, a palette, and a fine paintbrush.

Examples of primary and secondary colors. / An example of an analogous color palette. / An example of a color wheel.

Color wheel

There are 12 segments of the color wheel, starting with

Primary colors
Red, yellow, and blue cannot be made by mixing other colors.

Secondary colors
Orange, green, and violet are created by mixing two of the primary colors together.

Tertiary colors
Red-orange, orange-yellow, green-yellow, blue-green, violet-blue, and red-violet. Once you have mixed these colors, they form a circle, or wheel, as they go around infusing with each other. Other terminologies used to describe color are the following:

Tint
A pure color mixed with white; for example, red and white make pink.

Shade
A pure color mixed with black; for example, blue and black make navy blue.

Patina
The surface texture of the described color.

Tone
A general term to describe a tint or shade.

Hue
The position of a color on the color wheel.

Complementary colors
Pairs of colors that appear on opposite sides of the color wheel—for example, red and green, blue and orange, and yellow and violet.

Analogous colors
Those colors with a common hue that are adjacent on the color wheel—for example, blue-violet, violet, and red-violet.

Prada's Autumn Winter 2015–16 collection
uses a considered palette of colors
throughout.

Exercise 8
Color analysis

You have experimented with the color wheel and with mixing color. Now you can experiment further by mixing colors and analyzing the use of color for design.

Look to the research you have gathered so far for the previous exercises, and choose a color image that you find aesthetically pleasing. (Alternatively, you could just use a random color image for the purposes of this exercise.)

First, start experimenting with mixing the exact color, shades, and tones that are present in the image. You might need to mix several attempts until you get the color exactly right.

Then, when you have accurately represented the colors from your chosen image, choose 6 to 10 of the colors. Isolate these colors by cutting them out into squares or rectangles and placing them next to each other (but not sticking them down) onto white paper (white paper so that the background does not interfere with the perception of the colors). These colors will form your color palette. They should all work together as a set, and they will form the basis for the colors you will potentially use for your designs.

Then it is time to analyze the proportion of each color used in the image, because generally the colors will not be used in the same amount. Cut the colors into sizes that approximately represent the percentage/proportion used within the image. For example, blue might represent 50 percent; gray, 25 percent; beige, 17 percent; orange, 6 percent; and black, 2 percent.

Fabric

The selection of fabric for a garment is often essential to its success. It is both the visual and sensual element of fashion design. The weight and handle of a fabric determine the way a garment hangs and falls on the body. Designers often select fabric before designing a garment, gaining inspiration from the way it looks, feels, and handles. It may well be that you have sourced interesting textures and swatches of cloth during the research stage and can now start to use them in the development of a collection or garment.

It is important to note that the silhouette is often affected by the quality of the fabric used; for example, a silk jersey will naturally drape and flow around the body, whereas a heavier wool will have more structure and create more volume and shape.

Fabric selection is also about function and performance. In other words, is it fit for the purpose required? For example, denim fabric is used in jeans and workwear because of its hardwearing qualities, while Teflon-coated cotton is often used in rain-proof sportswear.

Fabrics often influence the season that is being designed for, as heavier-weight fabrics tend to be used in the autumn/winter and lighter weights in the spring/summer.

They are also selected for their aesthetic qualities—in other words, how they look, feel, and support the creative direction you have chosen, whether it be through print, texture, or embellishment.

When you start to use fabric in the design process, it is important to source different qualities, weights, and types so that you are not limited in the garments that you design.

Student sketchbook showing a range of fabric swatches.

Alexander McQueen Spring/Summer 2011 garment created using digitally printed silk satin.

"The selection of fabric for a garment is often essential to its success. . . . Fabric selection is also about function and performance. In other words, is it fit for the purpose required?"

Simon Seivewright

A student sketchbook showing swatches of various fabrics and techniques.

This look from Roksanda Spring/Summer 2016 uses layers of a lightweight fabric to create geometric frills. The raw and frayed edge of the fabric adds to the texture of the dress.

Fabric

Fiber

Fiber or yarn is the raw material out of which a textile is created. There are three main categories: animal (protein), vegetable or plant (cellulose), and mineral (synthetic). The fiber or yarn is then used to create fabric by either weaving or knitting them together.

Cellulose fiber

Cotton is a good example of a plant fiber or cellulose fabric. The soft "cotton-candy" fiber grows around the seed of the plant and is gathered, processed, and spun. It has versatile qualities because it can be woven and knitted and produced in many different weights—for example, denim cotton and cotton voile. It is naturally breathable and absorbs moisture well, which makes it a good cloth for hot climates or the summer season.

Protein fiber

Protein is an essential component of all living cells; keratin comes from hair fibers and is the most commonly used protein in the production of textiles.

Sheep and goats are the biggest suppliers of wool fleece, which is the raw product used to create woolen fabrics. Wool is a wonderful, warm, and slightly elastic fiber that can be woven or knitted to create cloth. Because of its natural origins, it is breathable and durable, and it can also be created in many different weights of cloth for different purposes, from tailored suiting to brushed mohair or angora for knitwear.

Silk is also a fiber derived from an animal—the silkworm. It is collected from the silkworm's cocoon, which is formed from the continuous thread that it wraps around itself for protection. Due to the way it is harvested, silk has always been a fabric associated with wealth and power. The fiber has luster to it and can be woven in many different weights and finishes.

Synthetic fibers

Synthetic fibers come in two forms: cellulosic and noncellulosic. Cellulose fibers are created by extracting cellulose from plants and trees and forming fibers such as rayon, Tencel, and acetate.

Noncellulosic fibers are created completely from chemicals and contain no natural fibers. These are known as synthetics and are composed of fibers such as Lycra, nylon, and polyester. The properties that these fibers can bring to fabrics are durability, stretch, and water resistance, and they are often used in sportswear.

They are perhaps best used when they are blended with natural fibers, such as a polycotton and a Lycra and wool mix.

Woven fabrics

Woven fabrics are created by interlacing vertical yarns (the warp) with horizontal yarns (the weft) at right angles to each other. The tightness and weight of the cloth depend on how many threads per centimeter there are and the thickness of the yarn.

Knitted fabrics

Knitted fabrics are formed by linked loops of yarn: horizontal rows are called courses and vertical rows are called wales. The elasticity of knitted or jersey fabric gives good stretch and draping qualities.

Nonwoven fabrics

Nonwoven fabrics are produced through the techniques of bonding and felting. Using heat, compression, friction, and chemicals, fabrics are created that do not fray, are waterproof, do not tear, and can be recycled. Leather and fur can also be classed as nonwoven fabrics although they are not synthetic.

Other fabrics

Other fabrics cannot be classified in any of the other areas and are essentially craft techniques, such as lace, macramé, and crochet.

Portobello market
fabric stall, London.

An embellishment by Martin Margiela Spring/Summer 2016 using unconventional components.

Print and embellishment

Print is a fundamental consideration in the design of a single garment or in the development of a whole collection. Print often illustrates the color palette, themes, and influences that a designer has been exposed to. Consider a collection inspired by constructivist art and art deco patterns and how these would inform color and pattern in the garments designed.

Print can be all over the garment in a repeat, it can be a motif in a more considered placement on the garment, or it can be engineered to fit the pattern pieces of the garment. New technologies in digital printing have allowed designers such as Peter Pilotto and Mary Katrantzou to fully exploit digital print in their collections and even feature it as their individual selling point, which is one way to stand out in the industry.

We discussed fabric embellishment, such as appliqué, smocking, beading, and embroidery, in chapter 1. Embellishment gives a three-dimensional and decorative effect to fabric, and can also help shape or create volume in the garment. In your research, you might have explored such techniques as sources of inspiration—for example, in early eighteenth century smocking or in African beadwork.

Simple but effective use of embellishment in Rick Owens's Autumn/Winter 2015–16 collection.

Givenchy Spring/Summer 2016.

Historic references

With so much dress history to look at, it is no surprise that many designers look to the past or to other cultures for inspiration. We have already discussed the importance of having an awareness of dress history and how it can provide valuable insight and design details for you to apply to your own creative ideas (see pages 16–17).

Using the information gathered in the research related to historical dress or even perhaps vintage clothing, you can now begin to analyze the elements of design that can be gained from this source. For example, you might look at historical silhouettes, construction details, proportion and line, fabric, print, and embellishment. You should now be considering all of these elements in the design of a garment and exploring a collection in relation to the historical content of your research.

Watteau-inspired evening dress by Vivienne Westwood, 1996.

Vivienne Westwood has used direct references to historical silhouettes, garment styles, and prints in many of her collections, most famously those based on the archives of the Wallace Collection and the French eighteenth century aristocracy. She has also drawn inspiration from paintings of period dress, referring to the artist Watteau and the women he painted as a source of inspiration. A slight note of warning should perhaps be sounded: while it is important to look at historical and cultural dress and costume, it should not be simply re-created, as to do so would move your work more into the area of costume design than fashion.

Remember: your task is selecting elements of the period source or country of origin and synthesizing them into something new, perhaps by mixing them with other references from your research or by altering the proportions, the placement, the use of fabric, or even the gender that the garment was aimed at.

Contemporary trends

We have previously looked at the importance of contemporary trends, through forecasting agencies, global and social interests, and even the bubble-up effect from street cultures. The research you have gathered may well contain some of this type of information, and as a designer, you need to have an awareness of what is going on around you and how it may affect your designs and ultimately the client you are creating the garments for. Using some of the trend information within your design work may well provide useful starting points for some of the design elements, such as color, fabric, or function.

Market levels in fashion

As a fashion designer, you must consider the market that you are designing for and where you see yourself in what is a very diverse and broad-ranging industry. Finding your niche or level will be an important development in your growth as a designer. Therefore, you should understand the different market levels and genres of the industry so that you can be a more successful designer.

Essentially, the two main approaches to garment design and production are *haute couture* (French for "high sewing") and *prêt-à-porter* (French for "ready to wear"). But, as with all industries, these approaches have subdivided over the years into a further series of levels that are more specialized and focus on specific target markets.

A Raf Simons design for luxury superbrand Christian Dior haute couture Spring/Summer 2015.

An outfit from Marc Jacobs's ready-to-wear collection Autumn/Winter 2015–16 collection.

Haute couture

Couture is the oldest form of designing and making clothes. It was and still is exclusive to Paris, France. The couture fashion shows are held twice a year in Paris, once in January and then again in July. They showcase to the buyers, specially invited clientele, and press the absolute top-end, one-off, most expensive, and often most creative and innovative designs that the couture houses have produced.

The industry supports a wealth of amazingly talented and skilled craftspeople from lace makers, beading and embroidery specialists, to highly skilled pattern cutters and seamstresses. Some of the most well-known design houses that still produce haute couture are Chanel and Christian Dior. "Newer" designers, who started out designing prêt-à-porter collections and now produce haute couture, include Valentino, Versace, Jean Paul Gaultier, Georgio Armani Privé, Maison Martin Margiela, Giambattista Valli, Viktor & Rolf, and Elie Saab.

Although very few people across the world are able to afford haute couture, it still plays a vital role in the industry, as it has few constraints on cost and creativity, and is often where ideas and aspirational ideals are first seen before they trickle down into the prêt-à-porter collections. Couture collections also act as advertising for other brand products such as cosmetics and leather goods.

Ready to wear/prêt-à-porter

The majority of the fashion-buying public cannot afford couture, and so the industry has developed a level of fashion called "ready to wear." The clothes are still made to a very high standard, but to a set of uniform sizes in much greater quantities. Whereas couture garments are made to measure to individual clients, ready to wear is essentially a wholesale operation. There is still a strong sense of design and innovation, as well as the use of beautiful fabrics and details. Many more companies are working, designing, and showing collections all over the world at this level of the industry and, unlike couture, there are more opportunities to show your collections because the ready-to-wear shows are held twice a year in the different fashion capitals of the world such as New York, London, Milan, and Paris, and in emerging fashion capitals such as Amsterdam, Dubai, Berlin, and Rio.

Luxury superbrands

Luxury superbrands are the giant global companies that have huge advertising budgets and are often part of a larger corporation which promotes and designs a wide variety of products throughout their own stores, such as cosmetics, perfumes, accessories, and furnishings. The ready-to-wear collections that they show are merely a starting point for the vast sales on additional products that they produce. The two main contenders at the superbrand level are LVMH (Louis Vuitton Moët Hennessy) and the Kering Group (formally PPR). Between them, they own such designer brands as Dior, Celine, Givenchy, Kenzo, Alexander McQueen, Stella McCartney, Marc Jacobs, Balenciaga, Bottega Veneta, Donna Karan, Louis Vuitton, Gucci, and Christopher Kane, to name but a few.

Mid-level brands and designers

A mid-level brand or designer is an established company with good sales and a high profile, but without the power of the superbrands. These brands are often sold through independent design stores or boutiques, department stores, and franchises around the world, and they may have their own stores as well. The mid-level designer will generally have a catwalk show and use it to promote a collection to buyers and the press. It is now also a trend for this level of designer to work with high-street brands to create more exclusive ranges based on their own collections, such as Viktor & Rolf, Lanvin, Isabel Marant, and Alexander Wang for H&M.

Independent designer labels

Independent designers work with a small team of people to produce a collection. They have total control over the design, sampling, production, promotion, and sales. The size of the business will determine how many of these tasks need to be dealt with in-house. The independent designer label sells wholesale to independent boutiques and department stores and shows through trade fairs and possibly through catwalk shows, too.

Casualwear and sportswear brands

Just as with the ready-to-wear designer market, superbrands exist within the more focused fashion design industry surrounding sportswear and casualwear, such as Nike, Reebok, and Levi Strauss. Just as with the superbrands, these niche brands can control a vast global market and can actually influence and impact upon every walk of life. The Nike logo has become one of the most recognized symbols in the world and is related not only to sportswear, but also to a lifestyle. There are also mid-level design brands, such as Diesel and G-Star.

High street

The high street has become one of the fastest growing and most diverse marketplaces in fashion design. Companies are able to react quickly to trends on the catwalk because of the way that their design, manufacturing, and quality developments are set up. Due to the quantities they produce, they can sell at much cheaper prices than designer brands. The high street in the UK is one of the most directional in the world, and stores like Topshop and H&M are fast becoming the favorite places for even the rich and famous to shop. Some of the larger high-street retail stores collaborate with ready-to-wear designers to produce exclusive ranges for them and, in doing so, offer that designer's brand name without the designer price tag.

Womenswear

The womenswear market is the most diverse and directional because women purchase clothing much more often than men in any one season and can be more adventurous in what they wear. Womenswear allows you to be more creative with styles and fabrics, and it is seen to be more glamorous. Because of this, it is overly populated with designers and superbrands, so it can be much more difficult, but not impossible, to make your own niche or client base within it as a designer. But because of the vast market and variety within it, you also are more likely to find employment.

Menswear

The menswear market tends to be more conservative, and although there are seasonal ranges, the changes tend to be subtler. Men generally don't buy into as many fashion fads as women and tend to have more classic pieces in their wardrobes. As a result of this, sales in this genre are fewer than in womenswear.

> "Men's fashions start as sports clothes and progress to great occasions of state. The tailcoat, which started as a hunting coat, is finishing such a journey. The tracksuit is just beginning one."
> Angus McGill, *National Geographic Fashion*

Childrenswear

Childrenswear design can be just as interesting and often follows similar trends to the main lines. Design brands such as Christian Dior and Versace all do lines in childrenswear. There tend to be more constraints than in the other genres, such as health and safety, and durability and function, especially in relation to clothing created for newborn children and toddlers.

Gender-neutral clothing

Designers and retailers are recognizing that women, men, girls, and boys need not be confined to traditional gender roles, and are responding to a society that is more accepting of those with gender fluidity. In spring 2015, Selfridges department store in London launched the Agender pop-up concept store selling unisex, androgenous, and genderless clothing, accessories, and cosmetics.

An Alexander McQueen menswear collection Autumn/Winter 2015–16.

Exercise 9

Design development

You have already begun to translate elements of your research onto figures to help with the early brainstorming of ideas. What this exercise shows you is how to get the most from these collaged figures and how to begin the process of design development or collection development.

In the collaged figures you produced in Exercise 6 (on page 103), you developed ideas mainly for shape and perhaps explored some quite abstract shapes on the body. What you now need to consider is how, through the addition of these other elements, a series of related ideas can be developed from just a few initial collages.

You need to think of design development as being like a family tree: all the ideas start from just a handful of key ideas. By adding and mixing other references and playing with the design elements, such as proportion, line, fabric, print, and function, you can generate a collection that has similarities yet differences.

Take three different collages from the early brainstorming exercise on figures (they are labeled A, B, C for this explanation):

A B C

Now design three variations of each collage. Perhaps add color and indicate a print, change a neckline, add a pocket, or change the function or type of garment. This will then give you three groups of ideas:

(Ax3) (Bx3) (Cx3)

Then from these new ideas that have similar qualities, start to mix across and see how the best elements from each grouping can affect the other:

(ABx3) (BCx3)

And then mix once more:

(ABCx3)

So from the initial three collaged figures, you have now drawn up 18 further design ideas, and all of them have a relationship or similarity to each other. This is essentially what design development or collection development is about—taking a set of known design elements and mixing them up to create a series or collection of garments.

You also can use this exercise with designs that have been drawn directly from your research.

Refinement of individual garments

Now that you have a basic understanding of design development, it is important for you to refine and develop more specific garments from the early experiments you have drawn. The collages and family tree ideas will help you explore different combinations of the design elements and hopefully provide you with a set of initial designs.

Refining your collection

You may have established a strong silhouette or line in some of your work, or perhaps the use of a color palette or prints was key to their appeal. It is these components that will remain the constant while you develop and further refine the collection.

What this next stage will achieve is to separate out the different types of garments, such as jackets and tailoring, knitwear and jersey, dresses, skirts, trousers, blouses and shirts, and outerwear. You can then begin to focus on the design variations on these specific types, because a strong collection should contain all of these types.

A designer often has a consistent silhouette and color palette throughout a collection, but through changes in garment type, fabric, use of print, and subtle changes to details, he or she is able to create many more outfits in the range.

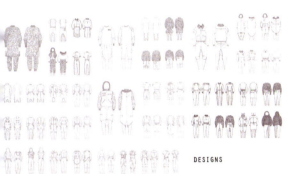

DESIGNS

A student sketchbook showing the selection of a color palette for a collection.

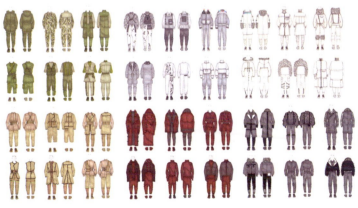

DEVELOPED DESIGNS

Exercise 10
Design development, part 2

Identify one garment type from the drawings you have already produced—perhaps a dress, for example.

Take this garment and start to design as many variations as you can—again using the design elements to help you with the development process. Consider changing necklines, hemlines, sleeves, collars, cuffs, fastenings, stitching, use of fabric, pockets, proportions and line, embellishments, and the possible use of print.

Remember to stay true to the original idea. This may well have been the silhouette that was created on the body in the initial collages.

You should be able to come up with 10 or 20 variations on this one garment, and if you then apply this method to all the other garment types, you can easily create a set of design developments into the hundreds.

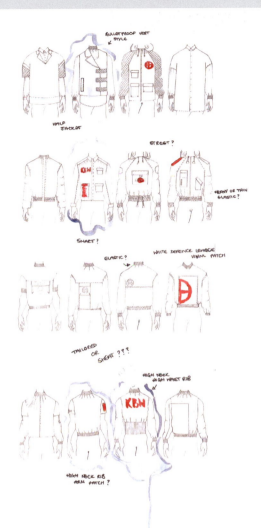

PRINT DEVELOPMENT

Student sketchbooks showing design development and refinement.

Selecting ideas to form a collection

By this stage, you should now have a clear vision operating throughout your designs. The key elements that you have worked with should be apparent and fully explored. Color, print, and fabrics should all be indicated and considered throughout the process of development and refinement, as well as styles and types of garment.

A good designer will produce hundreds of design sketches, with many variations and subtle detail changes, and will then have the task of selecting the strongest ideas to take forward into the final collection edit. It is this stage of the development process that is crucial to the overall success of a collection, because you will need to edit back your designs to create a coherent, well-balanced, and harmonious collection.

Unifying your collection

Identify the key pieces or your favorite elements of the collection. Is this the dresses, tailoring, jersey or knitwear, skirts, shorts, trousers, jackets, or outerwear? Initially, try to build on one piece for each of these types, although the season may determine the types of garments that are expected in the collection. You don't see swimwear in autumn/winter collections, for instance!

From these key pieces, you need to add in any other important design ideas—for instance, the same jacket or dress but created in several different fabrics. Print often plays a key role in unifying a collection and is generally seen in several incarnations—in a dress, a skirt, and a blouse, for example.

Portraying a silhouette is key to the harmony of a collection; it can be seen in many different garments, as can the details placed on them. These elements create running themes in the final edit and help establish the final look of the collection.

How many pieces or outfits should be in a collection? The number really depends on the size of the design company or budget, as the next stage of the process is pattern cutting, sampling, and manufacturing. An independent label may have the resources to create only 20 outfits in any one season, whereas Gucci or Christian Dior may have over 50–80 outfits in its catwalk presentations and the money and manufacturing to support them. Undergraduates, as a rule, produce 6 looks for their final collection, and postgraduate students might produce 8 to 12. As a new designer, you will probably be creating collections of 10-plus outfits.

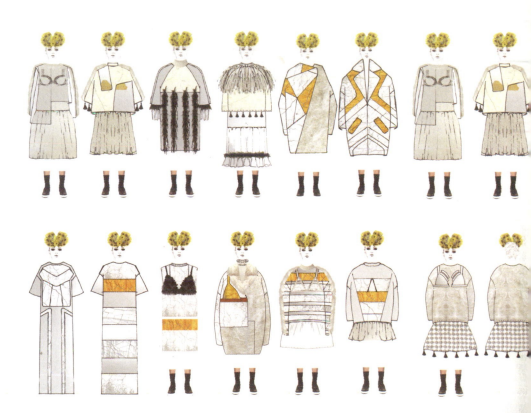

**Sketchbook showing
designs for a collection.**

Interview
WGSN

WGSN

WGSN is the world's leading trend-analysis and research service, providing creative and business intelligence for the apparel, style, design, and retail industries. WGSN's staff is composed of editors, designers, researchers, and journalists who travel continually, allowing them to deliver insight, inspiration, retail coverage, trend analysis, consumer research, and business information with a truly global perspective. This is complemented by local insight and intelligence from a network of experts based in countries across the world. This mix is the hallmark of WGSN and the foundation of its status as the foremost provider of strategic information. Launched in London in 1997, the company now has offices throughout Europe, Asia, Africa, South America, and the United States.

What role does WGSN have in the fashion industry?

Getting the right product into the shop at the right moment is a complex challenge, with many critical design decisions to be made far in advance. The insight and analysis that our experts provide helps our clients to navigate these complexities and develop their ranges effectively. In recent years, vast numbers of fashion and research images have become freely available online through social media platforms such as Tumblr and Instagram, making random fashion inspiration easy to come by. But for these "trend pixels" to become meaningful in a business sense, they have to be woven into a bigger picture, based on a solid understanding of the industry, and increasingly, actual data. WGSN can provide both. We have a separate product called WGSN InStock that provides data visualization and comparison shopping from e-commerce sites to help validate emerging trends and project them into the future.

How do you predict the trends so far in advance of the season?

It's a combination of straightforward analysis, experience, and intuition. In trend forecasting, you typically work on three seasons at the same time, four if you count retail. The pace is intense, but it gives us a great view of the bigger picture. Developing experience and good instincts is partly about constant exposure. If you spend a lot of time in the water and watch carefully, you learn how to pick up on the currents. These skills are particularly important for our seasonal trend forecasts, which look more than 18 months into the future.

How do you start the research process?

We start very broadly. Twice a year, content representatives from our global offices meet in London for WGSN Trends Day to discuss and share ideas on what we believe will be driving fashion and design trends in two years' time. We gather a large pool of research, including influences from art and design, architecture, film and photography, music, fashion and retail, as well as technology and consumer culture, and this forms the basis of our four seasonal Vision Trends.

Are the creative themes developed as a team? If so, who does what and how does it get collated?

Teamwork is key to the process. The Vision Trends are developed into a series of forecasts, with specific reports for womenswear, menswear, active sport, beauty, color, materials, textiles, and knitwear. Each forecast is run by a specialist team, but there is a lot of conversation and collaboration between these teams to ensure our trend messages are cohesive. They have to be accessible and inspiring as a whole, but also commercially relevant to their respective target markets. We are an online service, so most of the work happens in digital form, but physical mood boards are still useful for presentations and reviews across multiple categories or stories. You can only fit so much on one computer screen.

What kind of brief/constraints/ directions/markets do you work with?

Our client base is global and very diverse, both in terms of their markets and internal team structures. So we have to make sure we balance our content with the right mix of information, analysis, and inspiration. Our schedules are linked to events such as fashion weeks, trade shows, and product-development cycles, but the boundaries between seasons are becoming more fluid, and we often find that published information is used immediately, as everyone is trying to stay ahead of the curve.

How important is the research to the design process?

Everything we do requires research. There are peak times, but generally it never stops. It's not always as open and creative as at the beginning of the forecasts season; it can also mean spending hours or days looking at catwalk or street-style images for a big analysis report. Keeping up with industry news is part of the research, too. We need to know what's going on.

What advice would you give to anyone interested in a career in fashion/ fashion forecasting?

What we do at WGSN requires the skills of analysts, designers, photographers, journalists, and more recently data scientists, and we can find ourselves switching between these roles as needed. You need to be curious and observant, always looking for patterns or connections, able to think clearly, and communicate well, both visually and in writing. If you're versatile, you can learn a lot on the job, but because we are talking to a professional audience, it really helps to have industry experience and a solid foundation of knowledge in a particular area of fashion.

A selection of original WGSN CADs, artwork, and design assets available to download from the WGSN website.

Interview
Alan Oakes

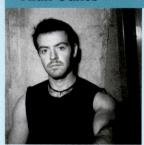

Alan Oakes is currently a conceptual, multidisciplinary designer and textile architect.

A trained architect, Alan has a BA in Architecture [minor in Art History] and studied Sustainable Design in Copenhagen, Denmark. He is a recent graduate of the MFA Fashion Design and Society at Parsons The New School for Design in New York.

The foundations of his design philosophies challenge the modern function of objects in all design fields/systems. In a society of increasing dematerialization, by altering the function of garment and transcending the user, Alan aims to inspire a new optimism within the possessions that fabricate the physical and mental architecture of dress. The most important, underlining factor in his efforts will always be the psychological relationship made between the user, space, and material substance.

How do you start the research process?
A process always begins with a question—in the context of design, the question challenges a problem. Through the investigation of this question, you develop a sort of dialogue that lends itself to a multitude of ideas all in hopes of answering the [currently] unknown predicament.

What kind of brief/constraints/direction/ market do you work to?
My work currently deals with the abstraction of consumer relation; investigating and challenging the psychological relationships between user, space, object, and communication.

Do you set themes? If so, how and where do you work?
My design process isn't driven by "themes" per se, yet an identity naturally develops as the process persists. By approaching my ideas without these attempts to define aesthetics, the value of the product overrides the objectivity. By refocusing the substance of work, I hope to render a product, feeling, or idea that is subconsciously understood by the user.

What are your sources of inspiration?
Inspiration lives in everything and is very uniquely processed by every individual. My process has nothing to do with imagery or "moods" necessarily, rather an initiation or exploration of personal cognition. I consider my emotions towards deciphering societal characteristics and problems to be of huge inspiration for my work—aiming to catalyze a functional response to issues needing consideration. As a fashion designer, we have huge responsibilities to offer users a skin. The conditions, to which these skins are produced, consumed, understood, and eventually disposed of is a holistic consideration in my work.

Do you have sources that you repeat or revisit in seasons or collections?
I attempt to approach projects or collections from a very pragmatic, yet abstract perspective. Allowing the work to exist in both a fine art and design realm—allowing it to stand as functional objects and communicated ideas.

Alan Oakes's designs at MADE Fashion
Week Spring/Summer 2015.

How important is the research to the design process?

The collections and garments or products that make up the coherence are mere by-products of my process, which for me, is of the upmost importance. Research and the process of investigation provide solidifying understanding of who I am as a creative person, craftsman, and artist.

Do you have a signature style?

I believe I have an identity within my body of work and process, but I don't necessarily agree with such terms. I believe designers should always be challenging themselves to evolve and create based on circumstantial needs—an idea that takes a chameleon's approach.

Do you ever design a collection with one person in mind?

I have designed collections in the past based on a muse or spirit that I find interesting for a specific reason. I find people very, very inspiring in terms of social and personal habits, and believe it's critical to analyze people when designing for just that . . . people.

How do you collate your research?

My research exists in many realms. I carry small notebooks with me at all times and write in them when the opportunity or idea presents itself. I get quite carried away by some thoughts and decide to then further investigate these abstractions, which then separately take a course of their own. They materialize into something physical or continue to be textual . . . there's never really a consistency to my approach, which keeps my process very invigorating for my personal interest.

How important is the marketing and promotion of a collection to its success?

I am still a very young designer, which provides a very difficult barrier to actually infiltrate public recognition without the aid or assistance of coordinators or public relation individuals. While advertising is essential for the mass communication of product or identity as a designer, I am approaching my work today as an artist in hopes of the work speaking for itself—a slightly naive approach, but also a great platform to provide further solving for future design efforts.

What advice would you give to anyone interested in a career in fashion?

Fashion today is an entirely different system than what once was. As the world quickly engages in social connectivity, a peak in consumption, materialization, and demand has changed the materialized psychology of how objects are understood and represent us as individuals and cultures at large. I believe any hopeful designer wanting to enter the fashion industry understands the responsibility that comes with the creativity they communicate through fashion—to whom and what it affects, and how important our decisions are as designers for either the prosperity of society or detriment. Fashion should not be treated as frivolously as I believe it is by the greater percent of designers and identities within the industry. The world is changing and a progressive understanding of fashion as a craft, creative process, and globalized industry is absolutely crucial for a sustainable people and environment of our world for tomorrow.

Interview
Study NY

Born and raised in Montreal, Canada, Tara St. James moved to New York City in 2004. She now calls Brooklyn home. St. James graduated in 1997 from LaSalle College School of Fashion Design in Montreal, one of Canada's top design programs, with a degree in menswear tailoring. Prior to graduation, she spent a year studying French art and literature in Toulouse, France.

After 10 years designing mens- and womenswear in both Canada and the US, Tara launched the New York–based label Study NY. Conceptual design and sustainability define this women's RTW brand. Study cuts and sews collections in NYC's garment district using both ethical fabrics and production methods. Many elements from the collections collaborate with artisans around the world; for example, locally sourced Peruvian alpaca is used in much of the knitwear.

Shortly after starting Study NY, Tara focused on educating the next generation of designers on the importance of sustainability in design. She has extensive lecturing and teaching experience in NYC. Some of the courses Tara has taught as a part of FIT's Sustainability Certificate include Corporate Social Responsibility, Supply Chain, and Sustainable Materials & Eco Labels. She has also critiqued and lectured at Parsons, Pratt, and FIT. Currently, Tara is working as Production Coordinator and Research Fellow in the Sustainable Strategies Lab for Pratt's new Brooklyn Fashion + Design Accelerator.

In 2011 Study NY was awarded the Ecco Domani Fashion Foundation Grant for sustainable design. In 2013 St. James's Anti-[fashion]-Calendar was named one of Sustainia100 Solutions for Sustainability—a global initiative spearheaded by Arnold Schwarzenegger to promote innovative global solutions across all industries. In 2014 Study NY was awarded runner up in the CFDA/Lexus Eco Fashion Challenge.

Tara St. James thrives on challenging her own preconceptions about design. Though vocal about her choice to use sustainable and ethical design principles for her label, Tara wants to be judged the same way all designers are judged, ostensibly for her design.

How do you start the research process?
I always start with fabric sourcing. Textiles are my greatest source of inspiration, whether it's a crisp whiting organic cotton shirting or a vegetable-dyed hand-woven denim, I usually find fabrics I love and want to work with first and then let them decide what shapes they want to take.

What kind of brief/constraints/direction/ market do you work to?
Working sustainably, or rather creating an ethical fashion brand, imposes an immediate set of constraints dictated by international regulations, laws, and my own set of beliefs and strategies. These create limitations—all very welcome ones—on the fabrics I can source, the production methods I use, and the types of garments I make. As a result I try to limit any additional constraints/markets in order to reach as wide an audience as possible.

Do you set themes? If so, how and where do you work?
Continuing the above sentiment, the only themes I tend to impose are those of zero waste strategies within the patternmaking process, and convertibility in the design process.

What are your sources of inspiration?
In addition to being inspired by the textiles I use, I also seek inspiration in art, reading, music, and daily living in New York City. One of the biggest influences on my work and my thought process is Sol Lewitt, whose art and concepts I greatly admire.

Do you have sources that you repeat or revisit in seasons or collections?
A physical source of inspiration I repeatedly visit is Dia Beacon in upstate New York. It's one of my favorite galleries in the world and houses a lot of Sol Lewitt's work.

Images from the Study NY Spring/Summer 2015 campaign.

How important is the research to the design process?

In my case research is the most important aspect of the design process. First textile sourcing research, then supply chain assessment to ensure the textile complies with at least one of my sustainability criteria, then research and testing to assess the quality and longevity of the textile.

What advice would you give to anyone interested in a career in fashion/fashion forecasting?

Be nice to everyone you meet and ask a lot of questions. You won't always get the answers you seek, but you'll never get them if you don't ask.

Do you have a signature style?

I like to think of my collection as seasonless—androgynous—oversized classic comfort—uniform but different.

Do you ever design a collection with one person in mind?

If I do, that person is usually me, or my mother, who is a huge source of inspiration for me. If I can answer the question "Would my mom wear this?" positively, then I know I'm on to something good.

How do you collate your research?

I used to create sketchbooks for every season, like mini portfolios where I included fabric swatches, color palettes, magazine tears and sketches, sometimes very detailed, of what I wanted to include in the collection. Unfortunately, I stopped this habit and have converted to Pinterest, which does not provide the tactile inspiration of a sketchbook.

Please discuss your brand Study and your approach to sustainability.

The name of the brand, Study NY, was born of a desire I had to really examine my production process and focus on a different technique every season. That began with zero waste patternmaking, then progressed to weaving, knitting, dyeing, printing, pleating, etc. Now that I'm no longer producing seasonal collections I still focus on different techniques, but I spread that focus over several months rather than each edition.

I have a checklist of sustainability tenets that I reference repeatedly. If I can check off at least three items from the list with each garment, then I will consider it sustainable and therefore eligible to be branded Study. But checklist aside, I don't believe another human, animal, or the environment should have to suffer for fashion. It's as simple as that.

This is the definition I find to be the most accurate: "*Sustainable means using methods, systems and materials that won't deplete resources or harm natural cycles*" (Rosenbaum, 1993).

A majority of my production is done in New York City's garment center. I use only organic or sustainable textiles (organic cotton, hemp, recycled poly, linen, and peace silk). I also work with fair trade and co-op-based factories in Peru and India who pay fair wages and work to sustain traditional weaving and knitting techniques while providing income for indigenous populations. Fashion is art in my opinion. But to some cultures, clothing is just a means of protection from the elements. There is such a huge gap between how first and third world nations view clothing and design. Ethical fashion has the ability to bridge that gap by providing developing nations with a market for their traditional craft techniques and a sustainable business opportunity.

What got you first interested in sustainability?

In 2004 I was working for a medium-sized fashion company sourcing in China and India when I was asked to start a new brand, which meant I had full control over the sourcing and production for the brand. When I started to find beautiful quality organic cotton textiles at mills in China, that prompted me to research the negative effects of conventional cotton, which ultimately led to more research on the effects of the industry as a whole on the environment and on people. I haven't stopped researching ever since.

Communicating your ideas

The ability to communicate your ideas and get what is in your head down onto paper is an essential part of being a fashion designer. In this chapter, we discuss the various approaches that you can use to render your ideas and designs. We also explore the use of mixed media and art materials, as well as how you can use them to illustrate different fabric qualities.

Design sketching is only one aspect of fashion drawing, and this chapter also analyzes the function of working drawings and the use of templates. Finally, it explores fashion illustration and the role it plays in the industry.

"Fashion illustration is one art form interpreted by another."
David Downton

Final collection presentation illustration, using drawing, collage, and Photoshop.

Drawing for design

Design drawing is about communicating your ideas. The ability to communicate your thoughts and designs is an essential part of being a fashion designer. It is not only a part of the development process, but also a way of explaining your thoughts to others. Although drawing is an important part of the design process, you do not have to be an excellent illustrator, drawer, or draftsperson, but obviously it does help.

Having a good understanding of the human anatomy—for example, muscular shapes, proportion, balance, stance, and skeletal structure—assists in the ability to draw and ultimately design more convincingly. One way you can develop this skill is to attend life-drawing classes, which are often run as evening classes at local colleges or adult education centers.

> ## "I don't design clothes, I design dreams."
> Ralph Lauren

Mark-making

Mark-making is the name given to the practice of using different art media and the methods of putting marks onto paper in a creative and expressionistic way.

Mastering your style through sketching

Another approach to developing your drawing is to sketch people on the move, perhaps walking past a café, on the subway, or in the street. Capturing people in motion and seeing how their clothes move and respond to the body are an important part of understanding how fashion can be drawn. In academic schools, fashion drawing and sketching are often given a lot of time and attention, because the ability to visually describe your designs and develop them through drawing with originality and personality is one of the fundamental parts of the design process. The design sketch must be figurative (in other words, it must vaguely resemble the human form), although it can be stylized and stretched to some extent. Long legs are an aesthetic to consider, as catwalk models tend to have long legs.

The sketch needs to describe the key design elements; therefore, it is important to draw not only the silhouette, but also the garment details, fabrics, print ideas, and colors. The sketch is the main tool used in exploring ideas. Rendering the figure many times over will allow you to play with the design elements in different combinations.

The design sketch itself should be something that is quick and allows you to get your ideas down rapidly. Your mind can move very quickly and wander off into different directions as you get more inspired by the research you have gathered. Speed often provides spontaneity and energy to your design work. Mastering your own style will also present uniqueness to your designs and add to the identity of the work.

Having basic skills in figure drawing and mark-making will always assist in the speed and accuracy of your rendered design work, but one tool that can help with this process is a fashion template.

Sketchbook examples of design sketching, incorporating textiles and further details of construction.

Templates

Fashion templates are predrawn figures that you can trace off through layout paper or tracing paper and then draw designs over the top. Templates allow you to focus on the design work and not on the figure. They also allow you to work quickly and in a more repetitive manner, perhaps working on the same type of garment many times until the strongest design appears.

You can find templates in most illustration fashion books, but where possible, it is best to try to develop your own figures to work on. This way, they will

be more individual and help you develop your own style and hand in fashion figure drawing.

The following example illustrates the development of a fashion figure through the different stages of development: from initially mapping out the proportions of the head, shoulders, waist, and legs to marking in the figure, then the garment shapes and details, and eventually the color and texture of the fabrics.

Here you can see how a basic design template is developed through a series of stages, considering proportion, balance, garment shape, color, and fabric rendering.

Exercise 11

Creating a design development six-figure template

As a designer, you need to develop and perfect your own style of rendering your design ideas. To facilitate this, you might create a template that allows you to work quickly and communicate specific garments or details to others effectively.

You can develop templates from life drawing, but you can also use collage and pencil outlines from magazine images.

For this exercise, create a lineup of six figures on an A3 landscape piece of paper (420 mm × 297 mm, or 16.54" × 11.69"). Why six? Well, you generally develop ideas across a minicollection of six outfits, so the ability to see all six outfits at once is essential to the selection of a cohesive and balanced collection. You should never really design an idea in isolation with only one figure on a page.

You need a retractable pencil, tracing paper, scissors, a glue stick, photocopies from fashion magazines, catwalk or runway shots, and access to a photocopier or computer with Photoshop software.

First, source some head-to-toe figures—preferably catwalk-type images—that give you front-on views. Look for back views, too. After you have found a good image, trace around the figure using a pencil and tracing pad, getting as much detail of the silhouette face, hands, and shoes as you can, but without too much detail of the clothes at this stage. An image from a swimsuit collection is ideal because it shows a lot of the figure with little clothing to distort the body silhouette.

You can also achieve this result by using a scanner and the drawing tool in Photoshop.

Photocopy the original photographic figure, and cut out the head and part of the arms, legs, or shoes. Glue them to your drawing (or do this in Photoshop); then stylize the head and face in your own hand, adding a strong individual dynamic through the use of mixed media.

You now have a template with a simple line-drawn outline of the figure, collaged with a photographed or stylized drawn head, face, hair, feet, shoes, and hands. How much of the original photograph to use is up to you. Photocopy this template five times, and stick all the figures side by side on one sheet of A3 landscape paper.

Photocopy this sheet, reducing the contrast of the drawn body line to a faint outline. Then copy as many figures as you need for drawing and collaging design ideas on top. (Do this using Photoshop and a printer if you wish to incorporate color into the figure's hair and face.) You can now design directly onto the template, adding garments, details, and simple color to the figures in flesh tones.

Because the outline of the figure is faint, you will not see the lines when drawing garments, but they will help you with proportions and maintaining a standard to the design work developed. These figures can then form the basis of your design development book/sketchbook; they can be bound to form a catalog of design that has been sequenced to develop various garment types, fabric and color permutations, and outfit combinations.

Illustrating with collage

We have already discussed using collage in both your research and early design work (see pages 76–77), but collage can also be a vital tool in rendering and illustrating your fashion designs. Working with a variety of mixed media and different paper qualities, in conjunction with components of your research, can provide an effective and original design sketch.

The use of collage also provides a freer and sometimes more expressive approach to the design process. Collage is best used alongside drawing at this stage because the details of the garments you've designed can be lost in the use of large pieces of photographic—perhaps more impressionistic—images.

LOOK FOUR

SPECS

Smoking Suit
Ottoman Overshirt

SMOCKED COAT

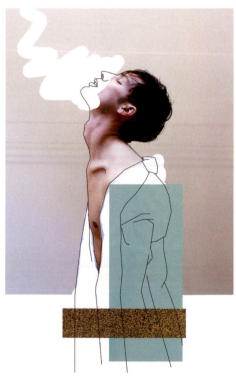

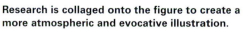

Research is collaged onto the figure to create a more atmospheric and evocative illustration.

Art materials

The use of a variety of art materials is important throughout the whole process of research and design because it allows you to explore your own hand and preferred choice of media. It also allows you to illustrate a variety of images and interpret them into new forms, patterns, colors, and textures. It is therefore essential that you equip yourself with the basics and understand how they can be used.

Examples of design drawing using mixed media.

Some basic art materials

Adhesive glue stick
Glue sticks are dry glue that is particularly useful for sticking paper, as it does not soak through in the same way that wet glue can. This glue is essential when using collage in your research and also in the experimental design stages. It does not dry immediately on contact and so allows you to reposition images when necessary.

Acrylic paint
Acrylic paint is water-based. It dries with the textures and brush marks created through application. It can have a slightly glossy look and can be used to render plastic and leather garments successfully.

Gouache paint
Unlike acrylic paint, gouache dries flat and with an opaque finish. It is slightly matt and chalky in finish. You can water it down to get a lighter shade or use it more thickly to get a darker shade, but it is more usual to mix and apply a lighter or darker tone at the same opacity. It is a good paint to block in even color and can be used with other media, such as oil pastels and colored pencils, to render different textures and fabric qualities.

Watercolor paint
Watercolor paint is a transparent paint used with water. You can buy it in tubes or in solid blocks that can be purchased as sets. It mixes well and takes on the characteristics of the paper it is painted on; for instance, used on colored paper, it takes on the color of that paper as a tint. It is great for illustrating more sheer and delicate fabrics because of its transparent qualities. Used with plenty of water, it dilutes to very pale and subtle shades. It works best on good quality drawing or watercolor paper.

Water-soluble coloring pencils

Water-soluble coloring pencils provide a quick and easy way to apply and mix color directly onto your drawings. Used dry, they can give the impression of texture and the weave of a fabric, whereas used with a little water and applied with a brush, they can be mixed to present a more transparent fluid mark.

Paintbrushes

Always invest in a good set of brushes in a variety of widths made from natural fibers, such as sable. They last longer and do not flare after use, which can make accurate painting difficult. Both flat and round heads are useful, as they allow you to make different types of brush marks and illustrate different details. Always wash your brushes thoroughly after use and remove all residue paint or ink.

Magic markers or brush pens

Magic markers or brush pens are superior felt-tip pens that come in a huge variety of colors and shades which often allow you to match up exactly to your color palette. They lay down color evenly and flat and also allow you to build up layers and darker tones. They can be expensive but are well worth the investment because they are the quickest and simplest way to put color accurately onto a design sketch. You also can use marker pens with other media such as colored pencils; they can often provide the base color to a fabric, with pencils providing the texture.

Fine-line pens

Fine-line pens come in a variety of thicknesses and are generally used in the rendering of designs and particularly working drawings, as they give a precise, graphic, and even mark.

Retractable pencils and lead

The retractable pencil is a reusable pencil in which you can replace and change the lead as it is needed. You can vary the grade, from hard 4H to soft 3B, depending on your requirements. For design sketching, it is best to have a lead that is anywhere from B to 3B, and in the pattern cutting room, it is better to have a harder lead, H to 3H. The benefits, apart from the ability to change the grade, are that you always have a sharp, precise mark, which is essential in design work.

Putty rubber

Putty rubber is a more moldable rubber than normal hard erasers. It can therefore be more precise for removing pencil marks and smudges.

Pencil sharpener

You need a pencil sharpener to sharpen normal pencils and watercolor pencils to achieve a clean, sharp mark on the page.

Layout paper

Layout paper is a slightly transparent lightweight paper used in the design drawing process. It is perfect for using with templates because you can just see through the paper; therefore, it allows you to trace a figure quickly and easily before applying the design work. You can purchase different types of layout pads; some work well with magic markers and stop the bleeding through to other pages. Because the paper is lightweight, it is not recommended that you use any wet media with it, as it tends to buckle and disintegrate.

Illustration

It is important to know the difference between fashion design sketching and illustration because the two play quite different roles. As discussed earlier in the book, design sketches are about the clothes: they show the silhouette, details, fabrics, print, embellishments, and color. They describe and show the clothing as it would be worn, they are generally in proportion, and they provide a visual tool to help the pattern cutter create the garment. They are also quick and can appear more spontaneous.

Illustration, on the other hand, is seen as an art form in itself, because it allows you to be even more creative with your use of media, and the quality of lines or brush marks that are laid out on the paper become more important and influential on the way the garments are perceived. Illustration is about evoking the mood of a collection and need not show the garments in full or even in a way that is obvious as to what they are. The work is much more expressive and stylized and often captures the spirit or even the character or muse that the collection was created for. The wide use of mixed media, digital, and Photoshop software can all be explored.

Final collection presentation illustration, using drawing, collage, and Photoshop.

Technical drawings, specs, working drawings

Technical drawings, specs, working drawings—or flats as they are often referred to—are the diagrammatical detailed drawings of your design work. They are the graphic, proportional, clearly drawn explanation of the garment, showing all the construction details, such as seams, darts, pockets, fastenings, and topstitching.

Producing your drawings

The flats are drawn with no figure represented, but to scale and—as the name suggests—in a flat rendering, with no indication of color, texture, or form. They also show both the front and back of the garment, something that is often forgotten in the design sketch. The working drawing supports the sometimes more fluid and artistic design sketch and must always be presented with the correct body proportions. It is generally the drawing that a pattern cutter uses to interpret a pattern from, because the design sketch can sometimes lead to inaccurate proportions. A working drawing is generally produced using either fine-line black pens or a clutch pencil, which uses fine leads. Different widths of fine-line pen can be used in the same drawing to illustrate different components; for example, a 0.8mm thick pen can be used for all the seam lines, darts, and details, whereas a 0.3mm thick pen can then be used to indicate all the topstitching, buttons, and fastenings.

Final portfolio illustration with technical drawings. Each garment is clearly represented with both front and back details drawn.

A technical drawing from the WGSN archive.

Exercise 12

Technical drawing by hand

This exercise is intended first as an observational exercise—examining an existing garment's proportions and details and how to accurately render them. Second, it is then about applying your observational skills learned through drawing an existing garment onto a garment that hasn't been realized yet—one of your designs.

You need a sharp pencil or retractable pencil (HB) and a selection of (black) fine-line pens (0.3/0.5/0.8mm), and some paper to work on.

Take an existing garment—preferably an outerwear garment because it is more complicated—and lay it out flat on a surface. Smooth out the garment until it is as flat as possible. Find the angle that the sleeves are at their most "comfortable"—that is, the angle where the sleeves lie away from the body of the garment with the least creasing.

Think about the proportions of the garment in front of you. You might even want to take down some measurements and scale them down to help with the drawing. The drawing needs to be as accurate as possible but does not need to be 100 percent accurate at this stage. Start to mark out the garment on the paper with pencil. This is a live drawing, and it can change at any time. Constantly cross-reference the drawing with the garment to check for accurate representation.

Once you have roughed out the shape in pencil, add in any details like pockets, collars, and topstitching. Again, cross-reference the drawing with the garment; use the placement of the details to help with the proportions and vice versa.

When you feel you have achieved an accurate drawing, you can use your fine-line pens to finalize it. To start, perhaps use the 0.5mm or 0.8mm pens for outline, seams, and details, and then the 0.3mm pen for topstitching and any other more delicate details.

Now that you have successfully rendered a technical drawing from an existing garment, try to apply the same thinking to one of your designs. Think about similar garment types and what they look like. You might already own something similar that you can use as a starting point for your drawing. Making a technical drawing for a design that doesn't exist yet will be difficult at first, but with practice and growing confidence, the technical drawings for your designs will improve.

Layout and composition

The layout and composition of your work greatly depend on how you have presented your designs. Most of the work you do will be contained in a sketchbook or on sheets of layout paper; these can then be bound into one presentation. The layout of a design page often requires you to work on figures in a series of groups—three as a minimum and up to six—in a row across the page and generally on A3-sized paper (420 mm × 297 mm, or 16.54" × 11.69").

This technique allows you to develop ideas across several figures at the same time and to immediately see any connections, running themes, or similarities occurring across the design. The layout therefore becomes much more simplistic and uniform as the design becomes progressively more important, eventually showing just rows of figures with the design applied to them.

The final part of the process

As the design becomes more selected and refined, the figures and their composition can become more complex and creative. Because the designs have been edited, you can spend more time on the drawing and rendering of the individual figures and designs. There are no hard-and-fast rules; whether you work in portrait or landscape format is up to you.

Line-ups and groupings of the final collection can be presented in a variety of ways and may be influenced by themes from the research and design process. Using different positions, stances, and styles of drawing, perhaps influenced by a period, can affect the final layout and look of the design work.

Using fashion magazines and photo shoots can help to suggest the positions of a final presentation. Figures sitting, standing next to one another, with one in the distance and one up close—these choices really come down to your own personal preferences.

Choosing the composition and layout of these selected designs is the final part of the process, and rendering the design work and considering the format are important parts of presenting this work. The creativity you have developed in the research and design process is now consolidated in the final designs and how you present them. Remember: your final presentation, first and foremost, should always be about the clothes.

LOOK THREE   LOOK FOUR   LOOK FIVE   LOOK SIX

A collection of figures used to develop ideas and identify connecting themes.

Beyond the drawing board

So far in this book you have learned about the importance of research and where and how to collate it, as well as its purpose in directing the design process.

So what happens next?

As with any product that has been designed two-dimensionally, it is essential that it is realized three-dimensionally so that you can complete any further developments and refinements before it is made up in the actual finished fabric or material. This first make is called a toile or sample. You need to have a basic knowledge of flat pattern cutting and garment construction to be able to understand how to transfer shapes and silhouettes onto the body from the design drawings that you have created. It takes designers years to perfect their skills and refine their ability to realize their drawings, so don't be disheartened if it doesn't work the first time around!

You may have already explored some three-dimensional ideas on a dress stand to gather information for designing, and these experiments may be a good starting point for pattern development. Modeling on the stand is a great way to learn about body shape and how flat fabric translates into form-fitting garments. Using these experiments can help to define an early paper pattern that you can refine and refit to the body until it starts to relate to the design drawings that you have created.

Technical drawings also provide a good and more precise interpretation of the sketches that you have created in the design process. They are generally what a designer uses to develop the precise paper patterns used in a toiling a garment.

Creating your first toile from a design or technical drawing shows you the merits of the shape and details that your garment possesses. It can then be altered and changed as needed, drawing on the toile itself, cutting and adding as needed. These changes can later be corrected on your flat pattern pieces and be subsequently retoiled if necessary. The whole process of moving your flat drawings into three-dimensional garments is fundamental to your success as a fashion designer. Without the understanding of the craft and skills of creating and working with a product, there cannot be a real understanding of how to design effectively.

Taking designs beyond the drawing board is something that all fashion designers should have a basic ability to achieve. Learning about cut and construction, as well as working with industrial equipment such as sewing machines, overlockers, and pressing machines will give you much more confidence in your ability to work within the industry.

> "Fashion is about change and about challenging what has gone before; it is about leading and not following; you should never feel that you cannot achieve your goals or push your design vision into the world."
> Simon Seivewright

Many good classes and self-help books can guide you through this part of the process, and as part of the curriculum, most full-time college and university courses in fashion design will teach you the skills you need.

Fashion requires you to have skills and strengths in many varied aspects of the design process. Being able to research and collate information is key. Processing this information to creatively draw and design ideas will need to come naturally over time; considering constraints and problems likely to be faced along the way is an inevitability that you should be prepared not to shy away from. Once you've mastered these strategic elements of the process, you will then have to consider yourself as both a designer and technician, and work with equipment and fabric to successfully realize your designs. Gaining all these skills takes designers years to perfect and refine until they reach a point of success and identity in the work they create.

A few final words. . .

With this book, you have started a journey of discovery, interest, and passion; and you now have the insight, skills, and knowledge to pursue your dreams. As with all creative endeavors, it will take time for you to perfect your abilities and to discover who you are and what you are about in terms of design.

All the great designers have had a strong personal signature to their work, and this can only be found through experimentation and exploration. Do not restrict yourself and never feel that you have seen and done it all. Good designers are driven to challenge themselves, to always look for the next new direction, and to constantly seek out further influences and sources of inspiration with which to stimulate their work.

Fashion is about change and about challenging what has gone before; it is about leading and not following. You should never feel that you cannot achieve your goals or push your design vision into the world. Good designers will constantly challenge themselves; will always look for new directions; and will seek out further-reaching influences, technologies, and sources of inspiration to stimulate and drive their work. Always remember: with practice and experimentation, anything is possible!

Enjoy your future career in fashion and good luck!

Interview
ThreeASFOUR

Recognized as one of the most innovative fashion labels today, threeASFOUR was founded in New York City in 2005 by Gabriel Asfour, Angela Donhauser, and Adi Gil, who hail from Lebanon, Tajikistan, and Israel, respectively. Having worked together since 1998 (under the label "As FOUR"), the trio uses fashion to promote the need for human coexistence and collaboration, and fuse technology with traditional craftsmanship. The collective shows twice a year during New York Fashion Week and has collaborated with numerous artists and musicians, including Björk, Yoko Ono, and Matthew Barney. threeASFOUR's designs are in the permanent collections of the Victoria and Albert Museum in London, the Costume Institute at the Metropolitan Museum of Art in New York, and the Palais Galliera in Paris. The trio won the Ecco Domani Fashion Foundation Award in 2001 and the Cooper–Hewitt National Design Award in 2015.

Please explain the philosophy behind threeASFOUR, the approach to working as threeASFOUR?
threeASFOUR is a real-life example of how different people from varied backgrounds and cultures can work together in harmony and understanding.

How do threeASFOUR start the research process?
We are three: One person starts and the other two follow.

What kind of brief/constraints/direction/ market do threeASFOUR work to?
threeASFOUR's core customer is a creative, intellectual individual. The brand appeals to specialty boutiques in major cities worldwide.

Do threeASFOUR set themes to the collections?
Each collection centers on a specific theme, yet there is a common thread weaving them all together.

What are threeASFOUR sources of inspiration?
threeASFOUR is fascinated with sacred geometry in nature and its dialogue with the human body.

Do threeASFOUR have sources that you repeat or revisit in seasons or collections?
We relentlessly imbue our creations with universal mathematic proportions.

How important is the research to the design process?
For threeASFOUR, research is not the main drive behind our creations—instinct usually takes over.

What advice would threeASFOUR give to anyone interested in a career in fashion/fashion forecasting?
You are a unique creative being. Be confident in your individual voice and it will be noticed.

ThreeASFOUR Autumn/Winter 2014.

Do threeASFOUR have a signature style?
Curvilinear construction and geometric tessellations.

What is the threeASFOUR design process?
Above all we seek balance between our energies. We function as a chosen family of three.

Do threeASFOUR ever design a collection with one person in mind?
Yes, we've done a few of those, from collaborating with Yoko Ono to working with Björk.

How do threeASFOUR collate the research?
Experience, accumulate, then edit.

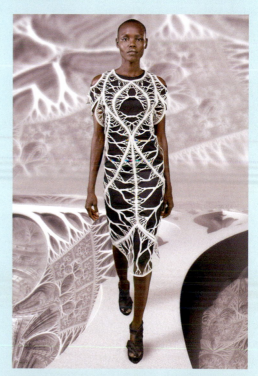

ThreeASFOUR Spring/Summer 2015.

Interview
Shelley Fox

Shelley Fox is the Donna Karan Professor of Fashion and the Director of the MFA Fashion Design and Society program at Parsons The New School for Design in New York. An award-winning designer, Fox has created numerous experimental and innovative collections that were sold internationally and have been included in prestigious exhibitions at the Victoria and Albert Museum, Design Museum, Barbican Art Gallery, Crafts Council, Institute of Contemporary Art (London), Modemuseum, Antwerp Landed 2001, FIT in New York, Design Museum Holon, and various British Council exhibitions that have traveled through Germany, France, Belgium, Poland, Lithuania, Czech Republic, Denmark, The Netherlands, Russia, Sweden, and Japan. Her work is published broadly in fashion, design, and art journals, as well as academic publications.

The Master of Fine Arts in Fashion Design and Society at Parsons The New School for Design is a highly selective program for talented, emerging designers, which was initiated through the support of alumna Donna Karan. Students develop their personal vision, with a focus on process and identity, through a body of work that encompasses highly executed, innovative clothing and accessory collections.

As a fashion educator, what is your approach to research within the design process, and what importance do you give it?

Every project we work on considers how to further develop the research process for the students' personal design approach. One project we have run since the launch of the program is an intensive course called Orientation 1, *Hole in the Map*. It is the first project they do. It is a good way of assessing how students think, take risks, and what their reaction is to a different way of thinking. We insist on no fashion outcome at the end of the project, which often throws them. The project consists literally of a map of New York City with a random hole placed within it, and each student receives a different map/hole which sites their research location for each of them. They are often coming to a new country, city, apartment, friends, and program, so it is a way of orientating and disorientating them at the same time. It is an intensive project where we hope to enable them to actually *see* when they *look*. It sounds so simple, but after many years of being in education, it's the one thing I witness year after year, and it's a global problem, not just a particular cultural or place. Students need to take initiative, stop asking "am I allowed?" If they haven't been pushed to research in depth, it's unfortunately something you still have to deal with at MFA level. We encourage the students to research like any designer would outside of fashion.

We are working on a new group project in the first semester, set around building their own vocabulary of clothing like an archive/encyclopedia. It's a complete experiment, but we didn't tell them before the briefing that we were going to photograph them all in the clothing they came to college in on that day and the project would be built off the back of that. It's fundamental in that we are now asking them to research their own clothing down to stitch count, fabrics, how it was made, its functional details, every single aspect and then build it out with historical references and associational references— "why do you wear it and why do you care about it or not?" Again we are trying to train them in looking in depth and why things are designed the way they are, and although this seems basic, it is amazing how many just don't look at clothes properly or think about them emotionally. I would argue that because they have such an oversaturation of images on the Internet that it is one of their main connections to clothing and that they seem unable to engage with clothing on an intimate level.

Braille Collection, Shelley Fox Autumn/ Winter 1998.

Having worked in education in both the UK and the USA, what are the differences, if any, in research and design philosophies?

I worked within education for approximately 10 years in the UK while running my own design label, Shelley Fox, from 1996 to 2007 and I have been the Director of the MFA program at Parsons in New York since 2008. For me personally, I don't see that there should be a difference particularly now that the system of fashion is so global and that the student population is more international. There isn't a huge difference certainly in the way I have approached it coming from the UK

and relocating to the US. It is who I am as a designer and educator. I don't build projects around markets per se because the world is too complex.

The MFA Fashion Design and Society program at Parsons is international in population and in its approach to collaboration. We work with companies such as Sophie Halette (Paris), Mokuba (Japan), Swarovski (Austria), Loro Piana, Olivo, Zegna Baruffa, Umbria Trade Association (Italy), among many others. New York City is central to the teaching, in that it brings so many opportunities to the program, students, and the way we are able to work within the studio. We are very engaged with the industry, with suppliers, factories, etc., and it is key to how the students navigate the world around them. I think one of the fundamental differences is that fashion courses in the UK were born out of art schools in the '50s and '60s. I consider my own training to be art school training with a focus on fashion and textiles. The history of immigration to the US, particularly to New York City from Europe in the nineteenth century, is fundamental to how the industry developed here and how that was linked to the assimilation of immigrants and the demand for clothing. New York City was once responsible for manufacturing most of the clothing that dressed the US population. This would have an impact on how design schools were developed. They may have had different starting points, but today globalization of the industry impacts everything from industry to education.

What are the differences in the approaches to research and design between under- and postgraduate studies?

I don't think they should be different in approaches to research, but we recognize that an undergraduate program needs to consist of fundamental teaching of skill sets as well as design thinking, but it's key to how those skill sets are taught. Skill sets such as pattern cutting, construction, textiles, etc., should always be through interesting design thinking projects in order to engage the students in the first place. Engagement is key. However, I am going to contradict myself and say that some of my best MFA students have come from architecture undergraduate programs both from the US. It really is a case-by-case situation when recruiting at MFA level because you are really looking at their talent as a designer as well as them as a person and what they can bring to the program with their own experiences.

What is the (design) philosophy of the MFA in Fashion Design and Society course at Parsons?

Fashion is a system that brings together material resources, human capital, and artistic vision in a single garment. And that garment's cultural reception, dissemination through the marketplace, and ultimate disposal involves an equally complex chain of activity. Students are encouraged to develop their personal vision, with a focus on process and identity, through a body of work that encompasses highly executed, innovative clothing and accessory collections. The program fosters experimentation, providing students with the design and research skills they need to become successful in the field, including a critical awareness for self-development and growth. We are trying to develop ideas people and better thinkers who are aware of the bigger picture.

Your collections were quite conceptual, very well received, and are still referenced. Personally, what are your sources of inspiration?

Inspiration has come from so many places—Braille, Morse Code, and documentary photography—almost too broad to list, but sometimes from actual fabric developments themselves. The physicality of a fabric can drive a collection—literally the burning of Elastoplast fabrics, burning of sequin fabrics, scorching of felt fabrics. Now that I think about it, there was a lot of destruction in fabric building. Each season was different in some ways—sometimes it started from a more abstract point of view because of a book I was reading at the time. *Between Silk and Cyanide* was

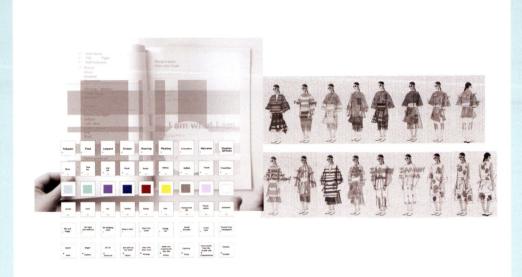

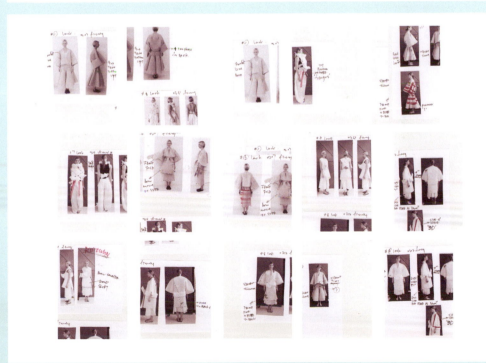

Andrea Jiapei Li, Design Development for Final Graduate Collection (Collection presented at New York Fashion Week, September 2014).

one book coupled with a trip to Bletchley Park around 1999–2000, which drove the ideas behind two collections at that time. Actually, a lot of the feelings and ideas behind the collections came from being based in Spitalfields and the east end of London in the mid 1990s onwards. Other project ideas have involved scientists, namely the *Nobel Textiles* project in 2008. I have always collaborated as a designer either with film, sound, communication designers, as well as artists. This notion of working was central to the building of the MFA program at Parsons.

How do you start the research process for a project?
I think it depends on the collection or project. When I was working on seasonal collections (I say that in the past tense as I don't run my label anymore), it would often be triggered by images that I had collected, which was always ongoing because you never stop looking at the things around you, books, films, etc., but it can be an accumulation of things. Sometimes I would use images that I had collected 10 years previous—I still have research files with images from nearly 20 years ago—they don't go away, but you just don't always use them at the time you find them. I try and instill this in my students—look, see, absorb, and collect—whatever it might be—your own photographs, your own experiences—you might not use it now, but it will always be there for you at the right time.

When I work on projects outside of seasonal collections, example being *AMU* with Random Dance Company, the research process was very different, as you work within a team of dancers, a choreographer, an artist, lighting designer, and composer. There are many elements that you are given to work with as well as the concept from the choreographer, Wayne MacGregor. This project started with the designers and dancers all having their heart scanned at the Brompton Hospital in London. AMU means *of the heart,* and the dance piece was built around this concept. When working with Michael Clark Dance Company on the project, *Oh My Goddess*, I would spend time at the rehearsals just hanging out with the dancers to get a sense of everything and the extreme movements. I love working with dancers.

How do you collate your research when working on your own projects?
I think I used to have too much research in the beginning and couldn't always focus. I think this was a lack of confidence in not knowing how to start the design development process. I have since learned that it doesn't have to be so complicated, but it's about researching something quite broadly in the beginning, narrow it down—work out what is really

important to you and begin to hone your idea—this can be through fabric development or something more abstract or about a piece of clothing but it's about pushing it forward. It's about not giving up, but also if you recognize something is not working but you have spent a good deal of time on it, then you need to walk away from it. It's not working, but you still learned something. I still have all my photocopies of *bandaging methods* from The Wellcome Trust when they were still in the old building in the late '90s; I realize now to spend time in a dusty old archive is an absolute pleasure and source of thinking space for the mind. That level of focus is exhausting but truly satisfying. I collect objects, imagery, make my own imagery through photographs (places such as Postman's Park in the east end of London is a favorite.) I still have an image of Spitalfields Church from about 1997 before it was cleaned. I realized that was decades of dust and soot cleaned away. There is something about capturing moments while you are in them even though you may not know how you are going to use them in the end.

Talia Shuvalov, Graduate Collection, May 2012 (Collection presented at New York Fashion Week, September 2012).

What in your opinion makes a good designer?

It has been evident that a good designer can communicate their work well to the outside world, or at least know how to communicate with their inner team to support them, a collaborator, and a team player even if they themselves are the director. Even when there are difficult decisions to be made and you are unsure where to turn and have taken on all the advice you can get, you also need to go with your gut. This has served me well on many occasions, and when I ignored it, then things went wrong, particularly when it involved making decisions on the people I worked with.

What would need to be considered by a new designer?

If it's a designer setting up their own label, then they need to build a team and hire people that are better at doing things that they are not so good at or that are not your strengths. You cannot be the holder of everyone's hands in your company. You need other people to shoulder the work and who are as committed to what you do as you are. If it's a designer going into a company, then they need to be a team player, want to learn everything so that they can build a full picture of what is needed. They will be working with many types of people and may not like everything they see, but they need to learn from it and build on it and be willing to be open to different ways of working.

What advice would you give to anyone interested in a career in fashion?

Commitment, because it's not an easy industry or profession and that needs to be said up front immediately. You will need to work hard—that's a given. If you want to be famous, first don't bother; the world is full of people who want that without the talent. Being recognized for your talent is different to being famous. Be open to working in different ways, learn from the best, be prepared to work from the bottom up. Be prepared to try interning in different areas when you are at the beginning such as design houses, magazines, assisting stylists, retail, etc., because you may realize that you don't want to be a designer, but your talent lies in buying, art direction, styling. The industry is huge, and there are so many roles that are creative. Do your research!

Andrea Jiapei Li, Graduate Collection, New York Fashion Week, September 2014.

Abstract A concept that describes an idea, feeling, or quality; not reality.

Aesthetic The quality of an object or design that depicts beauty or has a pleasing appearance.

Anchor points Points on the body that a fashion illustrator or designer uses to develop shapes or forms, such as the neck, shoulders, bust, waist, and hips.

Appliqué A technique in which a piece of cut-out fabric is sewn or fixed ornamentally to another fabric so as to create a surface decoration or pattern.

Beading The decoration of fabric with beads, usually sewn.

Brainstorming An activity in which all initial ideas are recorded quickly.

Brand A type of product made by a particular company, under a particular name that is widely recognized.

Brief A set of instructions directed at a designer, to outline the aims, objectives, and final outcomes.

Bubble-up Effect Fashion seen in street or subculture that influences designer fashion.

Client-based A product to be designed for a particular company or target market.

Collection A group of garments designed with certain features in common, such as color or shape.

Color wheel A spectrum of colors arranged in a circle to show the relationship between the colors.

Commercial A product that is intended to be bought by the general public.

Composition The way that visual elements along with text can be arranged on a page.

Concept board Another word for moodboard, which is a page or board where all the inspirational images are displayed.

Conceptual A vision based on ideas or principles.

Consumer analysis Collating information about the lifestyle of the target customer group, such as age, economic status, and occupation, which helps to guide the designer in creating commercially viable products.

Consumer behavior The analysis of consumer lifestyle and spending habits.

Contemporary Existing or happening now.

Contours The surface or shape of a garment or the body formed by its outer edge.

Costing What a garment costs to manufacture; this includes the raw materials and the making costs.

Critical path The time and process involved in creating a garment or collection, from concept to creation.

Cultural influences Relating to the habits, traditions, and beliefs of a society; or relating to music, art, theater, literature, etc.

Customization Making or changing elements of a garment to individualize the look or style.

Deconstruction Leaving the edges of a garment unfinished on purpose, or exposing seams on the outside.

Demographics Characteristics of a population regionally or nationally, usually in relation to their age, income, and expenditures.

Design development Initial design ideas that are modified into a series of design ideas that have cohesion.

Design drawing A communicative drawing of a garment that can be shown on a body or as a flat garment. It is different from a technical drawing, as it can be stylized.

Details The trimmings such as zippers and buttons, but can also refer to other components of a garment such as pockets, cuffs, and stitching.

Disparate Different in every way.

Drape techniques The way in which cloth folds or hangs as it covers the body or mannequin.

Dress stand A mannequin with standard measurements used to fit clothes on when not using a person.

Embellishment The application of components such as beads or sequins onto the surface of an existing fabric.

Embroidery The craft of sewing thread onto the surface of a fabric to create patterns and texture. By using different types of thread and stitch, you are able to create elaborate surface decoration on flat fabrics.

Fashion forecasting The process of predicting forthcoming trends.

Fashion illustration A drawing or painting of a garment or outfit, often represented on a figure, that communicates the mood of the clothes.

Function The purpose of a garment to meet specific demands.

Genre A style that involves a particular set of characteristics within a category of, for example, art, literature, or music.

Haute couture Originally a French term, meaning high-fashion, custom-fitted clothing. Literally means "high dressmaking."

Intellectual property Intangible property that is the result of creativity.

Journal A magazine or newspaper published about a specialist subject.

Juxtaposition The act of putting things that are not similar next to each other.

Layout The composition of a page or board.

Lustre The shiny or bright surface of a fabric.

Mainstream Lifestyle or habits adopted by the majority.

Mannequin Another term for the dress stand that clothes are fitted on; it can also refer to a model.

Market The business or trade of a particular product, associated with the sale of products.

Material Another word for fabric, but can also refer to other substances used to make clothes.

Merchandising department The department responsible for allocating and arranging garments creatively, for example, in window displays.

Model A person who wears clothes for a presentation, but can also refer to draping fabric.

Modeling Another term for draping fabric on a mannequin.

Moodboard A page or board where all the inspirational images are displayed; it can also include fabrics and trimmings.

Motif An identifiable pattern, design, or logo.

Muse An imaginary person or icon that gives a designer ideas and helps her or him to focus.

Narrative A story or a series of events.

Negative space The space around an object that can be used in composition to balance positive space.

Niche A specialized product group targeting a specific area of the market.

Palette A group of colors that sit well together.

Pantone Internationally recognized numbered shades and colors used throughout the creative industries.

Photomontage A montage or collage constructed from photographic imagery.

Pop art A type of modern art that started in the 1960s and uses images and objects from everyday life.

Primary research sources Findings that have been collected or recorded firsthand.

Print A flat pattern applied to the surface of a fabric using screens or by applying digitally.

Proportion The relationship of one aspect of a garment or outfit against another.

Punk Culture popular among young people, especially in the late 1970s, involving opposition to authority expressed through shocking behavior, clothes, hair, and music.

Recycle The reuse of a fabric, garment, or other materials and objects to create something new.

Research The creative investigation into a subject or the gathering of information.

Season Described in fashion terms as spring/summer or autumn/winter; usually fashion products are designed at least one season ahead.

Sensory Connected with the physical senses of touch, smell, taste, hearing, and seeing.

Silhouette The outline shape of a garment or collection.

Shade A pure color mixed with black.

Smocking A technique using stitch to gather fabric in a honeycomb pattern. There are many variations to this basic stitch, and it allows the designer to create shape and volume in a garment without the need to cut the fabric.

Specification drawing Also known as a spec drawing. This flat technical drawing of a garment uses line only and shows accurate proportions and details.

Storyboard Another word for moodboard, which is a page or board where all the inspirational images are displayed.

Structure The way a garment is made using seams and other construction methods.

Subculture A group of people who share similar customs, tastes, and ideas in, for example, music.

Superbrand A giant global company that produces a wide range of goods such as expensive luxury items.

Surface decoration The use of print or other embellishments on a fabric.

Surrealist/ism A cultural movement and visual art depicting unusual happenings or events, not based on reality.

Sustainability A quality of materials or processes that endure or have a low impact on resources.

Swatch A small piece of cloth used as an example of the color or texture of fabric or a sample.

Tangible research Physical objects that have been gathered as part of a body of research.

Target market The group of customers that a retailer aims to sell to.

Technical drawing A drawing of a garment in line only showing accurate details and proportions; also called specs or flats.

Template A drawing of a figure that is repeatedly used when designing.

Texture The tactile quality of a fabric or other material.

Tint A pure color mixed with white.

Toile A mock-up of a garment done in a cheaper fabric to test the fit and style before making in the real fabric. (Called muslins in the United States.)

Tone A general term to describe a tint or shade.

Topstitching Stitching that can be seen on the outside of a garment.

Trends Themes, colors, or ideas that are used by several designers at the same time incidentally.

Viewfinder A frame that allows you to conceal or expose part of an object or image.

Visual language An image created to communicate an idea using line, shape, color, texture, pattern, scale, and/or proportion.

Working drawing A technical drawing of a garment; also called specs or flats.

Youth culture The beliefs, practices, and style shared by a group of adolescents.

Zeitgeist German expression that means "the spirit of the times"; a general set of ideas, beliefs, or theories.

The Color Association

Beautiful colors with cool graphics. CAUS is the oldest color forecasting service in the United States. Since 1915, it has provided color forecasting information to various industries, including apparel, accessories, textiles, and home furnishings. In addition, assorted industry professionals comment on where they find inspiration and how it influences the direction of color. You have to become a member to get information.
colorassociation.com

Color Portfolio

Color Portfolio is a full-service color, trend, and communications marketing company. You can buy color presentation cards online. It also offers an offline service if you are looking for personalized design and concept development.
colorportfolio.com

Costume Gallery

Costume Gallery is an extensive site of 40,000 pages and 85,000 images aimed at students, designers, and those involved in textile manufacture and research.
costumegallery.com

Cotton Incorporated

Interested in textiles? In cotton? Check out this website for great information. Cotton Incorporated is a research and promotion company aiming to increase the demand for and profitability of cotton by providing value-added programs and services both in the United States and internationally for producers, mills, manufacturers, and retailers.
cottoninc.com

Ellen Sideri Partnership Inc

This consulting company provides trend analysis, color forecasting, brand design, retail store design, and web consulting.
esptrendlab.com

Fashion Monitor

This UK-based directory of the fashion industry with a global outlook includes details of fashion and style publications, PR agencies, and style and model agencies; it also provides daily fashion bulletins. This is a great source of industry information and jobs as well as contact details. This is a subscription-only service, but some educational institutions have licenses for students.
fashionmonitor.com

Fashion Net

This site gives you fashion news, designer bios, and runway shows and also has useful links such as fashion sites, online magazines, and designer sites. You also can buy and sell stuff on this website.
fashion.net

Fashion Windows

This great site has extensive listings covering fashion trends, runway shows, fashion reviews, designers, and models. Find the latest news and visuals from the fashion world as well as great information about visual merchandising. Some info available to subscribers only! Easy to use.
fashionwindows.com

Fashioning an Ethical Industry

Fashioning an Ethical Industry is a Labour Behind the Label project that works with students and tutors on fashion-related courses to give a global overview of the garment industry, raise awareness of current company practices and of initiatives to improve conditions, and inspire students—as the next generation of industry players—to raise standards for workers in the fashion industry of the future.
fashioninganethicalindustry.org

Global-Color

Global-Color is a forecasting company providing solutions to color selection in the fashion and interiors industries. Great information and inspiration for color. Easy-to-use format with nice graphics. Products are available to order online.
global-color.com

Le Book

Le Book is a good sourcebook for trends and inspiration for fashion designers, cosmetic companies, advertising agencies, art directors, magazines, photographers, fashion stylists, make-up artists, and hair stylists. It is for sale on the website. There is also a great list of contact names.
lebook.com

Moda Italia

Modaitalia.net's fashion search engine helps you find what you need from the fields of fashion, textiles, beauty, and lifestyle.
modaitalia.net

Nelly Rodi

This trend-consulting company is focused on colors, fabrics, prints, knits, lingerie, beauty, and fashion. Find a list of trend books on the website. In addition to its trends research, it offers communication services in publishing and organizing events. In French and English.
nellyrodi.com

Pantone Inc.

With its nice presentation and easy navigation, Pantone provides color systems and technology across a variety of industries. The company has products such as the color matching system, a book of standardized color in fan format. This is a reference for selecting, specifying, matching, and controlling colors in color-critical industries, including textiles, digital technology, and plastics. You can buy everything online.
pantone.com

Peclers Paris

The biggest fashion consulting company in Paris offers style and product, promotion, and communication consulting. Peclers trend books are very well known but may not be available to buy online in all countries.
peclersparis.com

Promostyl

Promostyl is an international design agency researching trends. Find its books and products for sale on its site. Offices are located in Paris, London, New York, and Tokyo.
promostyl.com

Sacha Pacha

This Parisian styling bureau caters to the fashion industry. It offers exclusive collection design and personalized trend consultancy. Sacha Pacha trend books are available for menswear, womenswear, and juniors here.
sachapacha.com

Styloko

Styloko is a UK network of sites fanatical about style, fashion, and shopping. A team of fashion-obsessed editors find and follow all the global trends, the best styles, deals and products, and deliver them in digestible portions. The main aim of this site is to bring together global fashion and local UK shopping.
styloko.com

Trendzoom

Previously known as Fashion Information, Trendzoom, a subscription-based website, is a great source for a view of international apparel trends. Reports for subscribers include updated catwalk trends and detailed illustrations, pictures, and color charts.
trendzoom.com

Visual Merchandising and Store Design

This site provides a subscription page and industry magazine for visual merchandisers, store planners, architects, designers, and interior designers. The information includes the latest techniques, technology, and trends along with design and trade-show coverage updates.
vmsd.com

Blogs and fashion magazines online:

AnOther Magazine / Another Man

A provocative digital offering by the creators of
AnOther Magazine and *Another Man* covering
fashion, beauty, art, photography, and informed
commentary.
anothermag.com

Business of Fashion

Business of Fashion combines fashion market
analysis and business intelligence, looking at
luxury brands, fashion pioneers, and new trends
in communication, marketing, and consuming
fashion, delivered in an accessible tone of voice.
businessoffashion.com

The Cool Hunter

The Cool Hunter celebrates creativity in all its
modern manifestations. It is a leading authority
on all things creative and a global hub for what's
cool, thoughtful, innovative, and original.
thecoolhunter.co.uk

Cool Hunting

This website has a global team of editors and
contributors who sift through innovations in
design, technology, art, and culture to create
their award-winning publication, consisting of
daily updates and weekly mini-documentaries.
coolhunting.com

Dazed & Confused

The online home of *Dazed & Confused* magazine,
featuring youth style, fashion editorial, music, art
and culture, social media trends, and all things
youth and digital.
dazeddigital.com

Garage Magazine

Garage magazine is a biannual print publication
focusing on high-profile collaborative projects
across contemporary art and fashion. Its online
presence is a great source of visual inspiration
and keeps you up-to-date with how the worlds of
fashion and art interact.
garagemag.com

i-D

i-D launched as a print magazine in 1980 and
now has an award-winning online presence.
Heralded as the scrapbook of the streets, *i-D*
continues to offer fashion editorials and reports,
music, culture, and social commentary to a
devoted audience of followers.
i-d.vice.com

Interview

Interview is an American monthly magazine
founded in 1969 by artist Andy Warhol and
British journalist John Wilcock; it describes itself
as "Conversations between some of the most
creative minds from the worlds of fashion, art
and entertainment." Originally celebrity focused,
Interview now features fashion editorials by
some of the world's best stylists, photographers,
and art directors.
interviewmagazine.com

It's nice that

Updated daily, this site features the latest cute,
cool, or creative ideas from all fields of art
and design. It now includes a biannual printed
magazine called *Printed Pages* and hosts a series
of talks and symposiums.
itsnicethat.com

Love

This fashion, style, and culture British biannual
magazine published by Condé Nast leads the
way in fashion editorials. The website is big on
visuals and fun, with coverage of fashion parties,
features, and backstage photos.
thelovemagazine.co.uk

Purple

The web version of this French print publication
is as provocative as the biannual printed
publication, covering fashion, architecture, art,
music, nightlife, and travel. Originally set up
as an antifashion, counterculture publication,
Purple is a well-established fashion and style
publication yet retains its irreverent attitude.
purple.fr

The Sartorialist

The Sartorialist has images of people on the streets of New York and Paris. The main focus is on the clothes that they wear and the shops that they inhabit. The street style imagery is supported by sharp and brief commentaries.
thesartorialist.com

Self Service

This Paris-based biannual magazine has high-end fashion editorial and interviews with the world's leading fashion luminaries. The website is a style leader and highly curated online accompaniment to the print publication.
selfservicemagazine.com

SHOWstudio

SHOWstudio is an award-winning fashion website, founded by fashion photographer Nick Knight. It works with the world's most sought-after filmmakers, writers, and cultural figures to create visionary online content, exploring every facet of fashion through moving image, illustration, photography, and the written word.
showstudio.com

Style.com

Style.com is a comprehensive fashion resource produced by Condé Nast. It hosts excellent coverage of collections, which can be searched by season, designer, and trend. The website features complete fashion show coverage (the videos and photos are online right after the shows), the lowdown on celebrity style, trend reports, expert advice, and breaking fashion news.
style.com

Style Bubble

Susie Lau's blog/website has become synonymous within the fashion industry as one of the first fashion blogs to be picked up by the mainstream fashion press and design houses. Her blogs from the front row provide quick and immediate access to the key shows of the season and showcase emerging talent.
stylebubble.co.uk

Trendland

Trendland is a fashion editorial dream! It showcases the latest (and older) editorials from every fashion magazine imaginable, and is constantly updating and enlarging this incredible archival resource.
trendland.com

V Magazine

V Magazine was launched in September 1999 as the younger sibling publication to the limited-edition quarterly *Visionaire*. *V* is large format and visually driven, and this applies not only to the print publication but also to the online version. News from fashion, music, and art as well as fashion editorials, videos, and online exclusive articles.
vmagazine.com

Vogue UK

Vogue Online is the web version of the UK monthly. It contains show coverage, daily news, interviews, and job opportunities.
vogue.co.uk

Vogue Italia

The Italian edition of *Vogue*, owned by Condé Nast, *Vogue Italia* is probably the most avant garde of the *Vogue* editions, with intelligent commentary alongside shows, trends, beauty, and celebrity. The online version also features student graduate collections.
vogue.it/en

WGSN

WGSN is Worth Global Style Network, which provides online news, trends, and an information service for the fashion and style industries.
wgsn.com

Wonderland

This online version of the glossy biannual fashion publication documents popular culture including fashion, art, film, music, and culture. It features both menswear and womenswear fashion coverage and commentary.
wonderlandmagazine.com

WWD

Womenswear Daily is the free online version of the American fashion retailer's daily newspaper. It offers headlines, classified ads, links to other sites, and subscription details, plus a preview of the full online version.
wwd.com

Bibliography

Baal-Teshuva J (2001), *Christo and Jeanne-Claude,* Germany: Taschen

Beckwith C and Fisher A (2002), *African Ceremonies,* New York: Harry N Abrams, Inc

Black S, ed. (2006), *Fashioning Fabrics: Contemporary Textiles in Fashion,* London: Black Dog Publishing

Bloom: A Horti-Cultural View, (February 2003) Issue 9, France: United Publishers SA

Blossfeldt K (1985), *Art Forms in the Plant World,* New York: Dover Publications Inc

Bolton A (2011), *Alexander McQueen: Savage Beauty (Metropolitan Museum of Art),* New Haven, CT: Yale University Press

Bolton A and Koda H (2012), *Schiaparelli and Prada: Impossible Conversations,* New Haven, CT: Yale University Press.

Borelli L (2004), *Fashion Illustration Next,* London: Thames & Hudson

Brand J and Teunissen J (2014) *The Future of Fashion Is Now*, Netherlands: Museum Boijmans van Beuningen

Brogden J (1971), *Fashion Design,* London: Studio Vista

Bruna, D. (ed.) (2014), *Fashioning the Body: An Intimate History of the Silhouette,* New Haven, CT: Yale University Press

Callaway N, ed. (1988), *Issey Miyake: Photographs by Irving Penn,* Japan: Miyake Design Studio, New York: Callaway Editions Inc

Charles-Roux E (2005), *The World of Coco Chanel: Friends Fashion Fame,* London: Thames & Hudson

Cole D (2003), *1000 Patterns,* London: A & C Black Publishers Ltd

Cosgrave B (2005), *Sample: 100 Fashion Designers, 10 Curators,* London: Phaidon Press Ltd

Currie N (1994), *Pierre et Gilles,* France: Benedikt Taschen

Dawber M (2005), *New Fashion Illustration,* London: Batsford Ltd

Diane T and Cassidy T (2005), *Colour Forecasting,* Oxford: Blackwell Publishing

Edmaier B (2008), *Earthsong,* London: Phaidon Press Ltd

Fukai A (2002), *Fashion: The Collection of the Kyoto Costume Institute: A History from the 18th to the 20th Century,* Germany: Taschen

Gallienne A and McConnico H (2005), *Colourful World,* London: Thames & Hudson

Golbin P and Baron F (2006), *Balenciaga Paris,* London: Thames & Hudson

Gooding M (1995), *Patrick Heron* (PB Ed.), London: Phaidon Press Inc

Gorman P (2006), *The Look: Adventures in Rock and Pop Fashion,* London: Adelita

Hamann H (2001), *Vertical View,* UK: teNeues Publishing Ltd

Hejduk J and Cook P (2000), *House of the Book,* London: Black Dog Publishing

Hillier J (1992), *Japanese Colour Prints* (1st ed., 1966), London: Phaidon Press Ltd

Hodge B, Mears P and Sidlauskas S (2006), *Skin + Bones: Parallel Practices in Fashion and Architecture,* London: Thames & Hudson

Holborn M (1995), *Issey Miyake,* Germany: Taschen

Itten J (1974), *The Art of Color* (1st ed., 1966), New York: John Wiley & Sons, Inc

Jenkyn Jones S (2002), *Fashion Design,* London: Laurence King Publishing

Jiricna E (2001), *Staircases,* London: Lawrence King

Joseph-Armstrong H (2000), *Draping for Apparel Design,* New York: Fairchild Publications, Inc

Klanten R et al, eds. (2004), *Wonderland* (2nd ed.), Berlin: Die Gestalten Verlag

Klanten R et al, eds. (2006), *Romantik,* Berlin: Die Gestalten Verlag

Knight N and Knapp S (2001), *Flora,* New York: Harry N Abrams, Inc

Koda H (2001), *Extreme Beauty: The Body Transformed,* New York: The Metropolitan Museum of Art

Koda H (2003), *Goddess: The Classical Mode,* New York: Metropolitan Museum of Art

Lauer D (1979), *Design Basics,* New York: Holt, Rinehart and Winston

Lawson B (1990), *How Designers Think: The Design Process Demystified* (2nd ed.), Cambridge: The University Press

Levi-Strauss C, Fukai A, and Bloemink B (2005), *Fashion in Colors: Viktor & Rolf & Kci,* New York: Editions Assouline

Malin D (2002), *Heaven and Earth: Unseen by the Naked Eye,* London: Phaidon Press Ltd

Martin R and Koda H (1995), *Haute Couture,* New York: The Metropolitan Museum of Art

McDowell C (2001), *Galliano,* London: Weidenfeld & Nicolson

McKelvey K (1996), *Fashion Source Book,* Oxford: Blackwell Publishing Ltd

McKelvey K and Munslow J (2003), *Fashion Design: Process, Innovation and Practice,* London: Blackwell Publishing Ltd

Nash S and Merkert J (1985), *Naum Gabo: Sixty Years of Constructivism,* Prestel-Verlag

Newman C (2001), *National Geographic: Fashion,* Washington: National Geographic Society

Parent M, ed. (2000), *Stella,* New York: Ipso Facto Publishers

Powell P and Peel L (1988), *'50s & '60s Style,* London: The Apple Press Ltd

Rock M, Prada M, and Bertelli P (2009), *Prada* (1st ed.), Milan: Progetto Prada Arte

Sorger R and Udale J (2006), *The Fundamentals of Fashion Design,* Switzerland: AVA Publishing SA

Stipelman S (2005), *Illustrating Fashion: Concept to Creation* (2nd ed.), New York: Fairchild Publications, Inc

Tatham C and Seaman J (2003), *Fashion Design Drawing Course,* London: Thames & Hudson

Wilcox C, ed. (2001), *Radical Fashion,* London: V&A Publications

Wilcox C (2004), *Vivienne Westwood,* London: V&A Publications

Wilcox, C. (ed.) (2015), *Alexander McQueen,* United Kingdom: V & A Publishing.

Wilcox C and Mendes V (1998), *Modern Fashion in Detail* (1st ed., 1991), New York: The Overlook Press

Wilson, A. (2015), *Alexander McQueen: Blood Beneath the Skin,* United Kingdom: Simon & Schuster

UK Contacts

British Fashion Council
www.londonfashionweek.co.uk
The British Fashion Council owns and organizes London Fashion Week and the British Fashion Awards. The BFC has close links with the UK's top fashion design colleges through its Colleges Forum, which acts as an interface between industry and colleges.

Fashion Awareness Direct (FAD)
www.fad.org.uk
This organization is committed to assisting young designers succeed in fashion by bringing students and industry together at introductory events. FAD fashion competitions provide young people with opportunities to further their creative and practical skills, integrate cultural research into their work, and showcase the results to the industry and media.

Fashion Capital
www.fashioncapital.co.uk
Fashion Capital aims to provide a one-stop online support resource for all areas of the clothing and fashion industry.

Fashion United
www.fashionunited.co.uk
Fashion United is the business-to-business platform for the fashion industry in the UK. It offers all fashion-related websites and information, the latest fashion news, and the Fashion Career Centre. The Fashion Career Centre lists current jobs in fashion, gives advice on applying, and provides a free newsletter subscription.

London Graduate Fashion Week
www.gfw.org.uk
Graduate Fashion Week was launched in 1991 as a forum to showcase the very best BA graduate fashion design talent in the UK.

US Contacts

Council of Fashion Designers of America
www.cfda.com
The Council of Fashion Designers of America, Inc. (CFDA) is a not-for-profit trade association whose membership consists of more than 400 of America's foremost womenswear, menswear, jewelry, and accessory designers.

The Garment District NYC
http://garmentdistrictnyc.com
The Garment District Alliance was formed to improve the quality of life and economic vitality of Manhattan's Garment District.

Pantone Color Institute
www.pantone.com

European Contacts

Modem
www.modemonline.com
This information resource gives an overview of both fashion and design from the European perspective.

Royal Society for the Encouragement of Arts, Manufactures & Commerce
www.thersa.org
The RSA's student annual awards scheme, Design Directions, offers a range of challenging projects that comment on the changing role of the designer in relation to society, technology and culture.

Careers/Work Experience Contacts Prospects

Prospects
www.prospects.ac.uk
The careers advice section is an invaluable resource for graduates looking to make the most of their degree and develop their career. Providing comprehensive, in-depth career advice for graduates of any subject, no matter what kind of career guidance you're looking for.

Fabrics and Trims

UK

Broadwick Silks
www.broadwicksilks.com

Cloth House
www.clothhouse.com

Kleins
www.kleins.co.uk

VV Rouleaux
www.vvrouleaux.com

US

M&J Trimming
www.mjtrim.com

New York Elegant Fabrics
www.nyelegant.com

Tinsel Trading Co
www.tinseltrading.com

Courses

UK

Central Saint Martins College of Art and Design
www.csm.arts.ac.uk

Kingston University
www.kingston.ac.uk

London College of Fashion
www.fashion.arts.ac.uk

Manchester Metropolitan University
www.artdes.mmu.ac.uk/fashion

Middlesex University
www.mdx.ac.uk

Northbrook College Sussex
www.northbrook.ac.uk

Nottingham Trent University
www.ntu.ac.uk

Ravensbourne College of Design and Communication
www.rave.ac.uk

Royal College of Art
www.rca.ac.uk

The Fashion Retail Academy
www.fashionretailacademy.ac.uk

University of Brighton
www.brighton.ac.uk

University of Westminster
www.westminster.ac.uk

Europe

Amsterdam Fashion Institute
www.amfi.hva.nl

Domus Academy
www.domusacademy.com

Flanders Fashion Institute
www.ffi.be

Hogeschool Antwerp, Fashion Department
www.antwerp-fashion.be

Institucion Artistica de Enseñanza (iade)
www.iade.es

Parsons Paris
www.parsons-paris.com

US

Academy of Art University
www.academyart.edu

Fashion Institute of Design and Merchandising
www.fidm.com

Fashion Institute of Technology
www.fitnyc.edu

Parsons School of Design
http://www.newschool.edu/parsons/

Rhode Island School of Design
www.risd.edu

Museums and Galleries

UK

Barbican
www.barbican.org.uk

Contemporary Applied Arts Gallery
www.caa.org.uk

Design Museum
www.designmuseum.org

Fashion and Textiles Museum
www.ftmlondon.org

Fashion Museum Bath
www.museumofcostume.co.uk

Natural History Museum
www.nhm.ac.uk

Royal Academy of Arts
www.royalacademy.org.uk

Tate Modern
www.tate.org.uk/modern

The British Museum
www.thebritishmuseum.org

The Crafts Council
www.craftscouncil.org.uk

The Victoria & Albert Museum
www.vam.ac.uk

US

Cooper-Hewitt, National Design Museum
www.cooperhewitt.org

The Metropolitan Museum of Art
www.metmuseum.org

The Museum of Modern Art
www.moma.org

Solomon R. Guggenheim Museum
www.guggenheim.org

Whitney Museum of American Art
www.whitney.org

Europe

Louvre Museum
www.louvre.fr

ModeMuseum Provincie Antwerpen (MoMu)
www.momu.be

Musée d'Orsay
www.musee-orsay.fr

Palazzo Pitti Costume Gallery
www.polomuseale.firenze.it

The Musée des Arts Décoratifs
www.lesartsdecoratifs.fr

Triennale di Milano
www.triennale.it

Japan

The Kyoto Costume Institute
www.kci.or.jp

Index

acrylic paint, 154
African tribal culture, 12, 13, 35
analogous colors, 115
analysis
    color, 117
    of research, 82–93
Animae magazine, 39, 40
appliqué, 13
architecture, 48–49
art galleries, 41
art materials, 154–155

Bach, Malene Oddershede,
    24–27
BA (Hons) Fashion Design, 28
Balenciaga, 52, 109
ballpoint pens, 75
Balmain, 48
beading, 13
Beckham, Victoria, 52
Bertin, Rose, 110
bias cut, 111
blogs, 38–39
books, 40–41
brainstorming, 22–23
brief(s)
    client-based, 2
    commercial, 2, 3
    defined, 2
    purpose of, 2
    types of, 2
British Airways, 3
brushes, 75, 155
brush-tip pens, 75, 155
"bubble-up effect," 18
Buddhist Punk, 64
Burberry, 112

casualwear, 130
cellulose fiber, 122
Chalayan, Hussein, 56
Chamberlin, Powell, and
    Bon, 49
Chanel, Coco, 33, 49, 50
Chapman, Georgina, 94–96
charity shops, 46
childrenswear, 131
client-based briefs, 2

collage
    on figure, 102–103
    illustration with, 152–153
    in sketchbook, 76–77, 93
color
    in design, 114–116
    in moodboard, 88
    in research, 9
    in research analysis, 82
color analysis, 117
colored pencils, 75
coloring pencils, 155
color wheel, 115–116
Comme des Garçons, 48, 110
commercial briefs, 2, 3
communication
    art materials in, 154–155
    collage in, 152–153
    composition in, 159
    drawing in, 148–149
    layout in, 159
    templates in, 150–151
complementary colors, 115
composition, 159
conceptual inspiration, in
    research, 34
Conté pencils, 75
Costelloe, Paul, 3
costing, in brief, 3
costume, as inspiration, 42–43
Courrèges, André, 56
Craig, Keren, 94–96
crinoline, 6, 7
cross-referencing, 80–81
cultural influences, in research,
    14–15
culture
    African tribal, 12, 13, 35
    Japanese, 15
    Mexican, 14
    street, 54–55
    youth, 54–55
customer, in brief, 3

deconstruction, 78
design
    collage in, 102–103
    color in, 114–116

contemporary trends
    in, 127
development elements in,
    108–114
draping in, 104–105
drawing for, 148–149
embellishment in, 125–126
fabric in, 118–123
function in, 113
historic references in, 127
ideal selection in, for
    collection, 136
layout paper in, 102
line in, 111–112
market levels and, 128–131
photomontage in, 106–107
print in, 125–126
proportion in, 111–112
silhouette in, 108–110
unification of collection in,
    136
details
    in design, 113
    in menswear, 113
    in research, 8
    types of, 113
development elements,
    108–114
Dior, Christian, 15, 17, 52, 110,
    114, 128
Dolce and Gabbana, 20
Doll, Lady Clapham, 42
Downton, David, 147
drapery, photomontage with,
    106–107
draping, 104–105
drawing. *See also* illustration
    for design, 148–149
    in sketchbook, 72
    technical, 157–158
    techniques, 74
    utensils, 74–75
    working, 157
Dr. Noki, 62–64

embellishment, in design,
    125–126
embroidery, 13

185

Acknowledgments

I would like to thank the following people for their help with this book (in no particular order): Matt Ryalls, Philip Clarke, Rob Currie and Sara Kozlowski, Karin Gardkvist, Nigel Luck, Ivan Moya, and Colette Meacher and Sophie Tann at Bloomsbury.

I would also like to thank everyone who agreed to be interviewed for this book: Malene Odderschede Bach, Paul Rawson, Dr. Noki, Christopher Raeburn, Marchesa, Nigel Luck, Volker Ketteniss (WGSN), Alan Oakes, Tara St. James, Gabriel Asfour, and Shelley Fox.

Thank you to the many talented students who lent their work: Marco Bajjali, Stephanie Birkett, Danielle Brindley, Thomas Brookes, Antonio Cascione, Dale Cloke, Danielle Collier, Hannah Ford, Roxanne Goldstein, Victoria Hicks, Pelin Isildak, Chloe Johnson, Halyn Kim, Keong Lee, Alice Loft, Arianna Mele, Olivia Overton, Alexander-Marian Tunsu, Rhiannon Wakefield, Jasmine K Wickens, Ning Xu, Xe Linn Yeap, and Mengya Zhao.

I would like to dedicate this book to the memory of Simon Seivewright; Simon and I were friends for twenty years, and it has been a great honor to work on this book and to continue his legacy. I would also like to dedicate it to Simon's husband, Gary Boxell, whom I admire greatly; and Simon's parents, Max and Diane; his sister, Alex, and family.

Last but no means least, I would also like to thank my husband, Gareth Williams, for always being there for me.

Credits

iii Photo by Victor Virgile/Gamma-Rapho/Getty Images

vi SIPA/REX/Shutterstock

viii Photo by GraphicaArtis/Getty Images

p05 Thomas Brookes

p06 Dover Press

p07 Photo by Ulrich Baumgarten/Getty Images

p07 Photo by David Crespo/Getty Images

p08 Photo by Antonio de Moraes Barros Filho/ FilmMagic/Getty Images

p08 Photo by Victor Virgile/Gamma-Rapho/Getty Images

p10 Photo by Antonio de Moraes Barros Filho/ WireImage/Getty Images

p11 Photo by Buyenlarge/Getty Images

p12–13 Olivia Overton

p14 Photo by Luis Acosta/AFP/Getty Images

p14 Photo by Francois Guillot/AFP/Getty Images

p15 Photo by Alain Benainous/Gamma-Rapho/ Getty Images

p15 Photo by GraphicaArtis/Getty Images

p16 Photo by Imagno/Getty Images

p17 Photo by Guy Marineau/Condé Nast/Getty Images

p18 Photo by Education Images/UIG/Getty Images

p21 Photo by 1645/Gamma-Rapho/Getty Images

p24 Photo by Helle Moos

p25 and p27 Photos by Rhys Frampton

p31 Photos by Claire Brand

p32 Photo by Kerry Dean

p34 Xe Lin Yeap

p35 Olivia Overton

p36 Mengya Zhao

p37 Pelin Isildak

p39 Animae Magazine

p41 Photo by Pool Simon/Stevens/Gamma-Rapho/Getty Images

p42-43 Victoria and Albert Museum, London

p44-45 (clockwise from top left) Photo by Taller de Imagen (TDI)/Cover/Getty Images, Photo by Subhendu Sarkar/LightRocket/Getty Images, Photo by Magdalene Mukami/Anadolu Agency/Getty Images, Photo by Independent Picture Service/UIG/Getty Images, Photo by Frank Bienewald/LightRocket/Getty Images, Farouk Batiche/AFP/Getty Images

p46 Photo by John Philips/Getty Images

p48 Photo by Antonio de Moraes Barros Filho/ WireImage/Getty Images

p48 Photo by Victor Virgile/Gamma-Rapho/Getty Images

p49 Photo by View Pictures/UIG/Getty Images

p50 Photo by Leon Neal/AFP/Getty Images

p50 Photo by Kristy Sparow/Getty Images

p51 Photo by Victor Boyko/Getty Images

p53 Photo by Edward James/WireImage/Getty Images

p54 Photos by PYMCA/UIG/Getty Images

p54 Photo by SSPL/Getty Images

p55 Photo by Thierry Chesnot/Getty Images

p56 Photo by Gareth Cattermole/Getty Images for IMG

p56 Photo by Victor Boyko/Getty Images

p58 Photo by Stuart C. Wilson/Getty Images

p58-59 Photos by John Philips/Getty Images

p60 Photo by Kirstin Sinclair/Getty Images

p62-63 Photos by Morgan White

p65 Photo by Nathan Pask

p66-67 Photos by Kerry Dean

p68 Chloe Johnson

p70-71 Alice Loft

p72-73 Richard Sorger

p74 Alexandru-Marian Tunsu

p76-77 Jasmine K. Wickens

p79 Photo by Kristy Sparow/WireImage

p80 Photo by Binder/ullstein bild/Getty Images

p80 Photo by Victor Virgile/Gamma-Rapho/Getty Images

p81 Jasmine K. Wickens

p83 Thomas Brookes

p84 Olivia Overton

p86 Rhiannon Wakefield

p87 Chloe Johnson

p88 Olivia Overton

p89 Jasmine K. Wickens

p90-91 Ning Xu

p92 Alexandru-Marian Tunsu

p93 Mengya Zhao

p93 Arianna Mele

p94 Photo courtesy of Marchesa

p95-96 Photo by Victor Virgile/Gamma-Rapho/ Getty Images

p97 Photo courtesy of Nigel Luck

p98 Diana Diaz

p98 Yutong Jiang

p99 Qiwen Wu

p100 Photo by Pascal Le Segretain/Getty Images

p102 Halyn Kim

p105 Jasmine K. Wickens

p105 Antonio Cascione
p107 Alexandru-Marian Tunsu
p109 Photo by Pascal Le Segretain/Getty Images
p110 Photo by Victor Virgile/Gamma-Rapho/Getty
   Images
p110 Photo by Pascal Le Segretain/Getty Images
p111 Richard Sorger/ Photo by Jez Tozer
p112 Photo by Henry Guttmann/Getty Images
p114 Photo by Pascal Le Segretain/Getty Images
p114 Photo by Victor Virgile/Gamma-Rapho/Getty
   Images
p116 Photo by Victor Virgile/Gamma-Rapho/Getty
   Images
p118 Olivia Overton
p119 Photo by Pascal Le Segretain/Getty Images
p120 Thomas Brookes
p121 Photo by Eamonn M. McCormack/Getty
   Images
p123 Photo by Matthew Lloyd/Bloomberg
p124 Photo by Pascal Le Segretain/Getty Images
p125 Photo by Richard Bord/Getty Images
p126 Photo by Edward James/WireImage/Getty
   Images
p127 Photo by Pierre Verdy/AFP/Getty Images
p128 Photo by Victor Virgile/Gamma-Rapho/Getty
   Images
p128 Photo by Antonio de Moraes Barros Filho/
   FilmMagic/Getty Images

p131 Photo by Ian Gavan/Getty Images
p133 Chloe Johnson
p134 Rhiannon Wakefield
p135 Chloe Johnson
p137 Olivia Overton
p139 WGSN
p140 Courtesy of Alan Oakes
p141 Photo by Mireya Acierto/Getty Images
p143-144 Courtesy of Tara St. James
p146 Alice Loft
p148-149 Alexandru-Marian Tunsu
p152-153 Olivia Overton
p153 Marco Bajjali
p154 Keong Lee
p156 Xe Linn Yeap
p156 Hannah Ford
p156 Alice Loft
p157 Antonio Cascione
p157 WGSN
p159 Olivia Overton
p162-163 ThreeASFOUR
p164 Photo courtesy of Shelley Fox
p165 Photo by Lon Van Keulen
p167 Andrea Jiapei Li
p168 Andrea Jiapei Li/Photography Monica Feudi
p169 Photo by Cara Stricker